Educational Research Primer

Other Educational Research titles:

Educational Research – Jerry Wellington

Educational Research in Practice – Joanna Swann and John Pratt

Doing Qualitative Educational Research – Geoffrey Walford

The Philosophy of Educational Research – Richard Pring

Quantitative Methods in Educational Research – Stephen Gorard

Reflective Practice in Educational Research – Linda Evans

Continuum Research Methods series

Action Research – Patrick Costello

Analysing Media Texts – Andrew Burn and David Parker

Ethics in Research – Ian Gregory

Research Questions – Richard Andrews

Researching Post-compulsory Education – Jill Jameson and Yvonne Hillier

Systematic Reviews – Carole Torgerson

Using Focus Groups in Research – Lia Litosseliti

Real World Research Series

Series Editor: Bill Gillham

Case Study in Research Methods – Bill Gillham

Developing a Questionnaire – Bill Gillham

The Research Interview – Bill Gillham

Educational Research Primer

Anthony G. Picciano

continuum
LONDON • NEW YORK

Continuum

The Tower Building   15 East 26th Street
11 York Road   New York
London SE1 7NX   NY 10010

First published 2004 by Continuum

British Library Cataloguing-in-Publication Data
A catalogue record for this book is available from the British Library.

Library of Congress Cataloguing-in-Publication Data
A catalogue record for this book is available from the British Library.

ISBN 08264 7202 8 (hardback)
      08264 7203 6 (paperback)

Typeset by YHT Ltd, London
Printed and bound in Great Britain by Cromwell Press

Contents

To individual researchers whose efforts have added to our understanding of the intricate nature of teaching and learning.

Preface

Many textbooks and other printed works are available on the subject of education research. Why then this primer?

In 1989, I was asked by the chairperson of my department at Hunter College in New York City to teach a graduate course entitled, *Seminar in Education Research Methods*. I examined the syllabus of the faculty member who previously taught the course and was surprised that little time was being devoted to statistics and quantitative methods. Qualitative research, ethnography, and descriptive case studies dominated the syllabus. My colleague, who was retiring, indicated that while he used to teach more statistics, other methodologies had become prevalent in the field, but more importantly, our students really struggled with quantitative approaches. I met with my chairperson and discussed with him my inclination to return statistics and quantitative methods to the syllabus. With his encouragement, I redesigned the syllabus to include four weeks of quantitative methods. While the students did struggle with the material, I believe its inclusion was necessary if they were to make decisions about their own research and if they were to develop the ability to read the published research of others.

During my first year of teaching the revised research methods course, I observed that most students understood the quantitative material during the session it was presented but a few weeks later they had forgotten it and needed a review. This is not an unusual phenomenon. However, the same forgetfulness was not as apparent with the qualitative material.

In the summer of 1990, having taught the *Seminar on Education Research Methods* for one year, I decided to develop a simple tutorial for the course and make it available to my students on a floppy disk. It was essentially a review of the course with an emphasis on the most difficult material. I encouraged the students to review the appropriate section after each class and added sections of the tutorial to the required reading assignments. Since then, I have regularly updated the tutorial and added new material. In 1996, rather than continue to make and distribute dozens of floppy disks each semester, I decided to create a website for the tutorial renaming it a primer. My students used the website as I had hoped but I also found that students in other colleges were using it as well. A week rarely went by that I did not receive an email from some student making a query or comment about the primer.

In 2001, I received an email from Anthony Haynes who represented The Continuum International Publishing Group in London asking me about writing a book on education research methods. When I asked how he came upon my name, he indicated that he had seen the website and was interested in converting it into book form. A couple of years later, Alexandra Webster of Continuum followed up on Anthony's initial contact and so here is the primer in printed form. I am most grateful to Anthony and Alexandra for their persistence and for giving me the opportunity to move my material from the Web to traditional book format. This is counter to much of what has been going on since the mid-1990s when writers and publishers throughout the world began moving their material from printed pages to electronic form. We now have the best of both worlds.

I also thank the incredibly competent staff at Continuum. Christina Parkinson solved a myriad of little problems that arose as we moved from manuscript to book. Sue Cope did a superb job of editing.

In addition, I have benefited significantly from my professional associations at Hunter College and the City University of New York. Especially important are the students and faculty in the Education Administration and Supervision Program, namely Janet Patti, Marcia Knoll, and Janell Drone.

Lastly, my children, Michael and Dawn Marie, help me to grow as a person in ways that they do not even realize. And Elaine, more than a wife, a friend, and a companion, cares for me and about everything I do.

ANTHONY G. PICCIANO

—1————————————

Introduction

————————————————

On March 29, 1989, N. L. Gage gave an address on the occasion of his receipt of the American Educational Research Association's Award for Distinguished Contributions to Educational Research. Gage, the Margaret Jacks Professor of Education at Stanford University, has enjoyed an outstanding professional career in education and psychology. During his address, he referred to educational research as a great battlefield upon which "paradigm" wars were being fought. A paradigm being a philosophical or theoretical framework of a scientific school or discipline within which theories, laws, and generalizations and the experiments performed in support of them are formulated. He made note of the antagonism between educational researchers who espoused a qualitative approach and those in favor of quantitative methods. He lamented that one school of thought considered highly complex human affairs such as teaching and learning impossible to study. He cited criticism that the use of the scientific method in educational research had been lacking. He expressed concern about the skepticism surrounding the role of educational research that emanated from both inside and outside the education profession. He concluded his address with a call and a reminder to the members of the American Association of Educational Research that:

> Educational research is no mere spectator sport, no mere educational game, no mere path to academic tenure. ... It has moral obligations. The society that supports us cries out for better education for its children ... especially the poor ones, those at risk, ... we must remember that the payoff inheres in what happens to the children. That is our concern. (Gage, 1989, p. 148)

Gage's comments are an appropriate introduction to the study of educational research. What is it? Why do it? How do you do it? What can it accomplish?

DEFINING EDUCATIONAL RESEARCH

Educational research is the seeking or searching for knowledge within the field of education. The word research derives from the French word "rechercher" meaning to travel through. The formal definition of educational research is a careful systematic investigation of, or "traveling through," any aspect of education. Educators should always be seeking to increase their knowledge and improve their understanding of the profession: the teacher about teaching and learning; the school administrator about leadership and school reform; the counselor about the social and psychological needs of children. The search for knowledge can be formal or informal and includes observation, gathering and analysis of performance data, individual case studies, and tightly controlled experiments. The search can be conducted by individual teachers, school principals, graduate students, professors in schools of education, or well-funded research organizations. The bottom line is that research helps us understand the education profession. Done for one's individual growth, it can be less formal and can rely on daily experiences, observations, and interactions. When done to be shared with other professionals or when presented to one's colleagues for their feedback and constructive criticism, it needs to be more formal. Indeed, if education is to be considered a profession with paradigms for building knowledge and understanding, the use of systematic methodologies is critical.

Understanding research concepts and being able to design a research project has specific practical benefits as well. Teachers and other educators seeking grants and external funding for their schools will likely need to provide an evaluation plan for determining how well the goals and objectives of the grant were met. A formal data collection and analysis process is usually the basis for such a plan and easily coincides with good research design principles. School administrators, in the present era of accountability and emphasis on verifiable learning outcomes, have come to rely on formal analysis of student test performance. In particular, data-driven decision-making processes based on quantitative research methods have become important techniques for planning and implementing instructional strategies for improving student performance. School counseling efforts have become far more complex in recent years as more and more students are in need of support services. Counselors must be proficient in interpreting diagnostic and standardized test results to determine appropriate programs for students with special educational needs, students who are bilingual, and students who need support for emotional, psychological, or social problems.

RESEARCH METHODOLOGIES

There is not complete agreement on the types of educational research methodologies that exist. The types that will be presented in this primer are as follows:

- **Ethnographic** – attempts to describe group behavior and inter-actions in social settings. It relies on qualitative techniques, especially observation and the careful recording of events and social interactions.
- **Historical** – attempts to describe and explain conditions of the past. It generally relies on qualitative data such as written documents and oral histories.
- **Descriptive** – attempts to describe and explain conditions of the present. It can be qualitative, such as in a case study or quanti-tative using descriptive statistics such as frequency distributions, contingency tables, and means. Descriptive research can rely on data gathered from a broad range of sources such as written documents, personal interviews, test results, and surveys.
- **Correlational** – attempts to explore relationships or make pre-dictions. It relies on quantitative data such as test scores, grade point averages, and results of attitudinal instruments, which can be correlated to show that some relationship may exist between or among variables.
- **Causal comparative** – also known as ex post facto research, attempts to explore cause-and-effect relationships where causes already exist and cannot be manipulated. It relies mostly on quantitative data sources such as written documents, interviews, and test scores.
- **Experimental** – attempts to explore cause-and-effect relation-ships where causes can be manipulated to produce different kinds of effects. It relies on quantitative data such as test scores and measures of performance.
- **Action and evaluation research** – attempt to determine the value

of a program, procedure, or product in a particular setting (e.g. school) with the goal of improving same. Action and evaluation research do not attempt to generalize results for a broader population.

All of these methodologies are legitimate but their use relates directly to the nature of the research problems that are being investigated. Each of these methodologies will be discussed in greater detail later in this primer.

PURPOSE

N. L. Gage spoke eloquently to the profession of the need to continually improve education for the good of children. Educational research has an important role to play in this improvement. The material in this primer seeks to provide the following:

- an orientation to the nature of educational research; its purposes, forms, and importance
- information which will help readers become more intelligent consumers of educational research: where to locate it, how to understand it, and, most importantly, how to critique it
- information on the fundamentals of doing educational research such as: selecting a problem, using available tools, and organizing a project.

ORGANIZATION OF THIS PRIMER

This primer is organized according to the basic educational research methodologies. After an examination of fundamental concepts such as the research outline, the scientific method, library resources, and basic tools in Chapters 2 and 3, each chapter thereafter will look at particular research methodologies, their rationales, and ways of conducting a research project using them. The last chapter provides guidelines for publishing and presenting research results. The primer also includes a substantive appendix of statistical procedures. Readers may wish to familiarize themselves with the material on statistical procedures first, and return to it as needed and as it is referenced throughout the primer. The primer concludes with a glossary of selected terms.

The educational research outline and the scientific method

Jean Piaget, born in Switzerland in 1896, was one of the most prolific researchers in the field of education and cognitive development. He received a doctorate in zoology in 1918 at the age of 22. His thesis was based on a study of invertebrates, specifically mollusks. In 1919, he went to Paris and studied pathological psychology at the Sorbonne where he also worked with Alfred Binet conducting research on children's reasoning and intelligence testing. He came to realize that his professional interest was in knowledge acquisition or the field of epistemology and embarked on a 60-year career of research and writing on the subject. He held several important positions including the directorships of the Jean Jacques Rousseau Institut in Geneva, the Bureau International Office de l'Education with UNESCO, as well as director and president of the Swiss Society on Psychology. His theory on the stages of cognitive development is well recognized throughout the world as a foundation for the understanding of how children learn. During his career, he used a variety of methods to conduct research. He supervised highly controlled sophisticated experiments with multiple subjects, observations, and formal testing. He also relied extensively on observations of small samples of children at play, eating meals, and at school. Boeree (1999) reported that Piaget poured two glasses of chocolate milk and sat down at a table with a single three-year-old child. Some of the chocolate milk had been poured into a tall skinny glass and much more milk into a short fat glass. The child reached for the tall skinny glass because the level of the milk was much higher than in the short fat glass. He concluded tentatively from this that a child at this age centers on one dimension and has difficulty discerning liquid volume. He repeated this activity many times with other children to verify his conclusion. Wadsworth reports criticism of Piaget's research which used simple observation, description, and analysis of children's behavior and which did not rest well with those committed to "American experimental procedures" (Wadsworth, 1996, p. 9). Nevertheless, Piaget made significant contributions to our understanding of inherently complex topics such as cognition, knowledge acquisition, and children's learning based on this type of research.

THE SCIENTIFIC METHOD

The scientific method is a procedure for problem-solving that is used in most disciplines. Jean Piaget used it throughout his career to study invertebrates, intelligence tests, cognition, as well as children's learning behavior. The scientific method consists of four steps:

- defining a problem
- stating a main question or hypothesis
- collecting relevant data
- analyzing the data to answer the question or test the hypothesis.

Paralleling the scientific method (see Figure 2.1), the educational research process consists of the following:

- **Identifying a problem** – the researcher selects a topic in which he or she is genuinely interested and then tries to establish why the problem is important and worthy of research.
- **Clarifying the problem** – the researcher reviews the research literature to determine what is known and what still needs to be known about the problem.
- **Formulating an hypothesis or research question** – the researcher states a specific hypothesis to test or posit a research question that he or she hopes to answer as a result of this process.
- **Developing a methodology** – the researcher selects an appropriate research methodology and implements procedures for collecting, summarizing, and analyzing data.
- **Reporting the findings** – based on data analysis, the researcher presents a clear statement of the findings.
- **Drawing conclusions** – using the hypotheses or research questions as the guide, the researcher forms conclusions based on the findings.

In educational research textbooks, this process is stated in different ways; what is important is that it stems from the scientific method.

Scientific method	Educational research process	Outline for a research proposal
Defining a problem	Identifying a problem	Statement of the problem
	Clarifying the problem	
Stating a hypothesis or main question	Stating a hypothesis or research question	Hypothesis/research questions
		Theoretical framework
		Review of the literature
Collecting relevant data	Developing a methodology	Methodology
Analyzing the data to answer the question or to test the hypothesis	Reporting the findings	Anticipated results
	Drawing conclusions	

Figure 2.1 Comparison of the scientific method, the educational research process, and the outline for a research proposal

SELECTING A TOPIC

Frequently the most difficult part of undertaking a research project is identifying what to study. Regardless of one's orientation (e.g., teacher, administrator, student-support professional), the possibilities are extensive. In recent years, a sample of popular research topics have included:

- school leadership and reform
- assessment and student learning outcomes
- instructional approaches
- diversity issues
- teacher preparation and support
- curriculum evaluation
- school finance
- class size
- policy studies
- use of technology in instruction
- family socioeconomics and learning
- parental involvement.

When selecting a topic, the researcher needs to understand his or her resources, especially finances and time. Ministries of education, federal and state departments, and private foundations invest millions of dollars each year in funding large-scale education research projects. Most of these dollars will go to research-oriented organizations, universities, and schools of education where teams of researchers have the expertise and wherewithal to carry out long-term projects with large sample sizes.

Most undergraduate and graduate students select topics that are much too broad. As a result, college faculty and mentors spend a good deal of time helping students refine and narrow their topics to projects that can be done by a single individual. In selecting a topic, an individual, especially if he or she is a student with limited resources, should consider the following:

- **Personal interest (to the individual researcher)** This is perhaps the most important consideration. The researcher must be truly interested in a topic to devote many hours in the library or on the Internet searching for, finding, and reading relevant material, then collecting data, and preparing a report.
- **Importance/Usefulness** The topic should be important and useful both to the researcher and to others in the education community. This does not mean that the topic must lead to major new discoveries but that other professionals will find it important enough to want to read about it.
- **Timeliness/Newness** The topic should be current and related to situations that are occurring in education. In recent years, technology-related topics in education have attracted a good deal of research because they are considered "state of the art."
- **Time** A careful assessment has to be made of the time (e.g., days, months, years) needed to complete the research.
- **Difficulty** Some topics are more difficult to study than others. For example, major decision-making, personnel practices, and certain experiments involving human subjects may be difficult to observe, to collect data for, or to get the requisite permissions to conduct the research.
- **Expense** A careful estimate of expenses, especially those related to travel, equipment, or materials, should be made.
- **Ethics** A researcher should always ask questions such as: Is this truly an objective inquiry? Is the researcher open to interpreting findings fairly and without prejudice? Is he or she looking to serve an individual, school, or larger political agenda?

While one or two of the factors above may be more important in selecting a topic than the others, they all should be considered together.

RESEARCH PROJECT PROPOSALS

Researchers frequently need to develop a proposal for their research projects. Students, grant seekers, and doctoral candidates develop proposals that are reviewed by faculties, funding agencies, or mentors. Proposals are generally organized to reflect the educational research process described earlier:

- statement of the problem
- hypothesis/research questions
- theoretical framework (optional)
- review of the literature
- methodology
- anticipated results (optional).

We will examine each section of the proposal and comment on its nature and importance to the overall research project.

STATEMENT OF THE PROBLEM

The statement of the problem serves as the introduction to the study. It should be a clear direct succinct statement of why the research is being conducted. Reference should be made to articles, books, authorities, or statements made by government officials that support the importance, usefulness, or timeliness of the research. The statement may also include any personal story or anecdote that provides the reader with further insight into the importance of the topic to the researcher. The conclusion of this section should be a declarative statement that begins: "The purpose of this study is ..." For example:

> The purpose of this study is to examine the learning outcomes of children enrolled in a pre-kindergarten program.

The length of the statement of the problem depends upon the purpose of the proposal. A statement of the problem in a research proposal for a grant or a dissertation may be longer than for a journal article submission.

HYPOTHESES/RESEARCH QUESTIONS

The hypotheses or research questions provide specific information about what the researcher intends to study. A hypothesis is a supposition or tentative conclusion, without proof, that will be used to guide the research. It is a statement of opinion of what the researcher expects to find. Hypotheses can be stated in two ways. A research or directional hypothesis is stated positively. For example:

Students who begin school in a pre-kindergarten program will perform better academically in later years than students who begin school at the kindergarten level.

A null hypothesis or nondirectional is neither positive or negative and assumes a neutral position. For example:

No difference exists in academic achievement in later years for students who begin school in a pre-kindergarten program as opposed to those who begin at the kindergarten level.

While a hypothesis can be stated either way, the null or nondirectional form may be more appropriate for certain statistical procedures. This will be discussed in greater detail at the end of this primer in the review of statistical procedures.

Research questions are also legitimate vehicles to guide research, especially exploratory research. Research questions tend to be less specific than hypotheses and leave open an extension of the research depending upon the findings. For example:

Is there any difference in the academic achievement in later years of students who begin school at the pre-kindergarten level versus the kindergarten level?

Using a research question also allows the researcher to use several sub-questions such as:

Is there any difference in the academic achievement in later years of girls versus boys who begin school at the pre-kindergarten level versus the kindergarten level?

Multiple hypotheses or research questions are acceptable and depend upon the nature of the problem being studied. In any case, for most educational research, the hypotheses or research questions should be conceived from the onset. They can be refined as the research evolves.

THEORETICAL FRAMEWORK

The theoretical framework is a general or overall theory which explains or helps one understand the context of the problem or phenomenon to be studied. Examples are:

- Theory of cognitive development (Jean Piaget)
- Theory of multiple intelligences (Howard Gardner)
- Theory on the limits of rationality in administrative decision making (Herbert Simon)
- Social system theory on student drop-out behavior based on Durkheim's theory of suicide (Vincent Tinto)
- Social systems theory of organizations to explain organizational behavior (Jacob Getzels and Egon Guba).

A theoretical framework is usually optional and not a required section in a research proposal. If a theory has helped guide the researcher's thinking or approach to the problem, then it should be included. There are, however, certain research projects such as doctoral level theses and dissertations that may require it.

REVIEW OF THE LITERATURE

The review of the literature is a critical component of any research project and should commence as early as possible in the process. A researcher needs to know what others have already studied and concluded with respect to the topic or problem at hand. In education, where so much research has been undertaken, this can be a very time-consuming but necessary part of the research project. In undertaking the review, the researcher should consider how the study will complement or "fit in" with other studies on the same topic.

In reading other studies, the researcher should look to answer several questions. First, are the findings consistent? If after a review of a number of articles the findings are generally consistent, then one must ask whether another study is needed. It is possible that an additional study could provide a new perspective because of a different sample of subjects, a different environment, or a different time period. This is a decision that the researcher has to make. If the findings from the research literature are inconsistent, then this gives credence to the need for additional study.

Second is the question of when research was done on the topic and whether findings have changed over time. If it is a topic that has been studied for many years, have there been changes in the findings? And, most importantly, what has the current (last three years') research found about the topic?

Third, what type of methodology or research procedures have been used to study the topic? Is there consistency in the type of methodology used? If so, why? If not, why not? These questions should give the researcher important insight on how to select an appropriate methodology for his or her own study.

A fourth consideration in reviewing the literature is to determine which studies tend to be cited frequently in other research reports. In a good review, the researcher will be able to identify the benchmark studies that provided important new knowledge on the topic. The findings from these benchmark studies can be most useful for framing a new study.

As the review of the literature proceeds, a researcher might come upon a meta-analysis of a topic. A meta-analysis is a study wherein a set of statistical procedures is used to summarize the results of a number of independently conducted research studies. While there are several statistical techniques for conducting a meta-analysis, one of the more popular ones uses effect size. Effect size is calculated by taking the difference in the means of two groups (e.g., an experimental group and a control group) and dividing it by the standard deviation of the control group. This procedure is more fully explained in the review of statistics at the end of this primer. If located, a meta-analysis can be very valuable to a researcher because it provides an extensive bibliography of existing research while also providing a combined analysis of the results of a number of studies. Unfortunately, meta-analysis is a very time-consuming undertaking and many topics in education have not been analyzed using its techniques.

METHODOLOGY

Depending upon the type of research to be done (e.g., ethnographic, historical, descriptive, correlational, causal-comparative, experimental, action, evaluation), and the nature of the problem, different approaches can be considered. Decisions are made regarding data needs, statistical procedures, samples, and test instruments. Much of the remainder of this primer will be devoted to the nature of research methodologies and their appropriate use.

As part of the methodology, the researcher should also identify or define any key terms that have not already been defined in the other parts of the proposal. Key terms may be any terms or acronyms (e.g., IEP – Individual Evaluation Plan, SLT – School Leadership Teams, SBM – School-Based Management) that have a specific technical meaning. Key terms may also include a definition of a commonly used term that will have a specific definition in the proposal such as "academic achievement as defined by student scores on a [specific] standardized test."

ANTICIPATED RESULTS

This section is optional and provides a brief summary of what the researcher might expect to find. It should be an objective statement of possible results.

A FINAL COMMENT ON THE RESEARCH PROPOSAL

As indicated earlier in this chapter, developing a research proposal is generally required when the project is a part of an assignment (e.g., thesis, dissertation) of an academic program or comprises the request for a grant. However, even when it is not required, developing some of the elements of a proposal is a good way to plan a project. The proposal might also be used to share one's plans with a colleague or two in order to get some feedback and suggestions for how to proceed.

Resources and tools for doing educational research

In the 1930s and 1940s, Kenneth and Mamie Clark, a husband and wife team of social psychologists, conducted a series of studies on the effect of race on black children's sense of self identity. The tools they used were relatively simple and included dolls, sketches, drawings, and crayons. For example, they showed the children, ages three to seven, four dolls, two of which were brown and two of which were pink, and asked them to make choices such as: "Give me the doll you would like to play with"; "Give me the nice doll"; or "Give me the bad doll." Another test involved giving the children sheets of paper on which were uncolored drawings of a leaf, an apple, an orange, a girl, or a boy. They would give the children a box of 24 different colored crayons and asked them to color the drawings. The Clarks specifically asked the children to assume that they were the girl or boy in the drawing and to "Color the [girl or boy] the color you are." Or they would ask the boys to "Color the girl the color you would like the girl to be" and ask the girls to "Color the boy the color you would like the boy to be." The Clarks conducted these studies in a number of cities and towns including Washington D.C., Boston, Philadelphia, and New York and invariably a substantive percentage of the black children selected light (white, pink, or yellow) colors rather than dark (brown or black) colors for the boys and girls. Marian Radke and Helen Trager conducted similar tests with black and white children in the early 1940s using cardboard cut-out colored dolls. Their results indicated that 57% of the black children and 89% of the white children preferred the white cut-out dolls (Kluger, 1975, p. 319).

On May 17, 1954, Chief Justice Earl Warren issued what many people consider the most significant decision in the history of the United States Supreme Court. In Brown v. Board of Education, the Court struck down state-mandated segregated schools in the United

States. In a footnote, Chief Justice Warren cited seven works by contemporary social scientists that helped guide the Court's decision. First, on the list was a paper entitled "Effect of prejudice and discrimination on personality development," by Kenneth Clark. In this paper, Clark used his and his wife's research as well as the research of others, including Radke and Trager, to support his views on the effects of race on black children. With Brown v. Board of Education, the United States began to deal with its racial issues, a process which is still continuing today.

In this chapter, an examination is made of the resources and tools that are used in educational research. These resources and tools range from the simple to the complex and include: primary and secondary resource materials; library resources; electronic resources; data-collection tools such as surveys and questionnaires; and data-analysis aids such as statistical computer software programs.

PRIMARY AND SECONDARY RESOURCE MATERIALS

Once a topic has been selected, a researcher spends a good deal of time collecting source material. The two major types of source material are primary and secondary. Primary source materials are any original documents, reports, official records such as student transcripts, attendance records, policy statements, and artifacts. For certain types of methodologies such as ethnography, descriptive case studies, and historical research, researchers try to gather as much primary source material as possible. In years past, primary source materials were frequently paper documents but today they may be records stored in electronic or computerized forms. Student records, census data, and test scores are now available electronically. Except for materials that are in the public domain, such as the United States census data, researchers need permission from school or other authorities to access the data regardless of their (paper or electronic) form.

Secondary source materials are documents, articles, descriptions, and reports done by individuals not directly associated with the data. Generally secondary data sources include analysis or interpretation by individuals "outside" the school or original source organization. Even though secondary sources are not first-hand material, they are still very valuable and frequently can lead the researcher to some of the best primary resources on a topic as well as provide excellent overviews, and reviews of the relevant research. When accessing secondary source materials, the researcher should always try to understand the perspective and point of view of the author. For example, an article on the use of standardized testing to measure student performance might have a different point of view depending upon whether the author is a teacher, a school principal, a representative of a teachers' union, or a national or state education department official.

For further information on primary and secondary source materials, the following Websites are highly recommended:

Yale University Library
http://www.library.yale.edu/ref/err/primsrcs.htm
University of California at Berkeley Library
http://www.lib.berkeley.edu/TeachingLib/Guides/
    PrimarySources.html

LIBRARY RESOURCES

The library houses vast collections of materials that are cataloged and sorted for easy access. Increasingly, this material exists in both paper and electronic form. While many researchers spend hours going through card catalogs and book stacks, they are more likely to be using computer databases and search engines to find relevant material. The transformation, during the latter part of the twentieth century, of data and information processing to high-speed high-volume computerized database systems combined with ease of access via data-communications technology (e.g., the Internet) has made information searches far more effective but not necessarily less time-consuming. A researcher might spend less time accessing material but more time sifting through it to determine its value and appropriateness. It is not unusual to use a search engine to locate articles on a particular topic and receive in excess of a thousand "hits." Researchers must become proficient in using search engines to refine requests and can do so with practice. Researchers must also be familiar with the databases that are available in their fields. In education, ERIC (Education Resource Information Center – see Figure 3.1) is by far the most popular; a researcher should become familiar with its database collections as well as its keyword or identifier system.

ERIC provides two major indexing systems. The *Current Index to Journals in Education* (*CIJE*) allows users to access abstracts and full citations of articles published in over 800 recognized educational journals. Once the abstract of an article is located, the researcher can

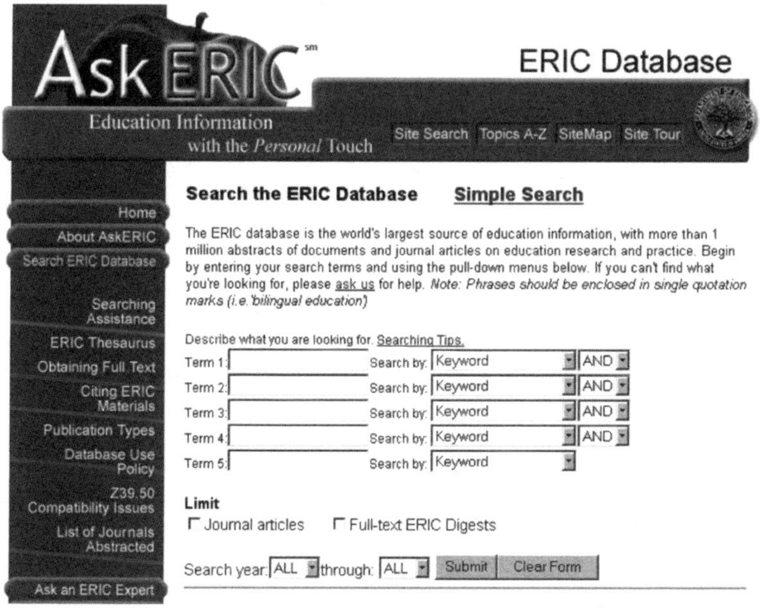

Figure 3.1 ERIC (Education Resource Information Center) website

use the citation to locate the actual article in its print or, if available, electronic form. ERIC does not provide full-text articles for *CIJE* entries. ERIC also provides a second indexing system, *Resources in Education* (*RIE*) for reports, studies, monographs, and papers that have not been published. These are materials submitted to ERIC by the authors for inclusion in the indexing system, in some cases, with free license to make the materials available to researchers. When a document is located in the ERIC *RIE* index, an abstract and instructions for acquiring the entry are provided. ERIC also provides additional database and indexing services beyond *CIJE* and *RIE* with which educational researchers should become familiar.

Besides ERIC, libraries will have other source materials that are of value to an educational researcher. A number of abstracts in education and other related fields are routinely available including:

British Education Index
Business Education Index
Canadian Education Index
Digest of Educational Statistics

Dissertation Abstracts International
Education Abstracts
Education Administration Abstracts
Educational Technology Abstracts
Multicultural Education Abstracts
Psychological Abstracts (PsycINFO – Online Version)
Reading Abstracts
Social Sciences Citation Index
Wilson Education Index (Online with Full Text Entries)
Sociological Abstracts

Libraries also maintain collections of yearbooks, reviews, and handbooks on specific topics and areas of study which are updated periodically. Examples of these include:

Handbook of Educational Psychology
Handbook of Research in Education Administration
Handbook of Research on Early Childhood Education
International Handbook of Bilingualism and Bilingual Education
International Journal of Educational Research
International Review of Education
National Society for the Study of Education Yearbook
Review of Educational Research
Yearbook of Adult and Continuing Education
Yearbook of Special Education

Experienced researchers develop expertise with the titles, databases, and handbooks in the topics and areas they hope to study. Those unfamiliar with these materials or new to research should schedule a visit with a reference librarian who will be more than happy to review them and provide valuable advice.

ELECTRONIC RESOURCES

Many published materials are available in electronic form. The electronic forms of these materials generally go through the same review processes as the printed versions. However, with the tremendous growth of the Internet and the World Wide Web, a good deal of material is being made available that has not necessarily been subject to a review process. Government agencies, professional organizations, research centers, and advocacy groups are making extensive use of the Internet to provide information about educational issues that might be of importance to researchers. This is a desirable aspect of the Internet; it is a free information resource, available to anybody with access to an electronic workstation. On the other hand, since much of the material on the Internet is not subject to review, almost anybody can publish information on the World Wide Web without regard to quality, honesty, or accuracy. Unscrupulous individuals use the Internet to publish inaccurate if not misleading information, the motivation for which is beyond the scope of this primer. As more researchers use Internet search engines such as Yahoo, Google, and Alta Vista, caution must be taken to make sure that the material is accurate. The old refrain "make sure you know who your author is," is doubly true for World Wide Web materials. With ease of access, anybody can publish anything at minimum cost for all the world to see.

With the above cautions in mind, the Internet nevertheless is a wonderful resource for gathering information on a topic. Using any of the simple search engines mentioned earlier, a researcher can easily locate valuable information. Various government agencies such as the US Department of Education and the US Census Bureau maintain websites containing entire databases of useful information. State education agencies likewise provide a host of information services on policies, finances, student demographics, and student performance that can be most useful to the researcher. Centers and professional organizations such as the American Education Research Association, the International Reading Association, and Phi Delta Kappa International provide access to materials that likewise may be useful. Figure 3.2 contains a sample of governmental agencies, centers, and professional organizations that provide information helpful to the educational researcher.

TOOLS FOR DATA COLLECTION

Many tools are available to the researcher for collecting data. Visits to school settings to observe instruction, structured interviews with educators, examination of student records, surveys, tests, and searches of Internet databases such as the International Archive of Educational Data or the US Census are some examples. All are appropriate depending on the nature of the study. A researcher will decide how to collect data based on the research methodology selected to study the problem. An ethnographic study of student behavior in a class usually requires a visit(s) to the natural setting or classroom. A correlational study of the relationship between parent involvement and academic achievement would require accessing

---

http://www.aasa.org
American Association of School Administrators

http://www.aera.net
American Education Research Association

http://www.cedu.niu.edu/blackwell/
Blackwell History of Education Museum

http://www.crede.ucsc.edu
Center for Research on Education, Diversity, and Excellence

http://www.cgcs.org
Council of Great City Schools

http://www.edweek.org
Education Week

http://ericir.syr.edu
ERIC/AskERIC – Clearinghouse

http://www.icpsr.umich.edu/IAED/
International Archive of Education Data

http://www.icpsr.umich.edu/
Inter-university Consortium for Political and Social Research (ICPSR)

http://www.fpg.unc.edu/ncedl
National Center for Early Development and Learning

http://www.nea.org
National Education Association

http://www.pdkintl.org
Phi Delta Kappa International

http://www.dfes.gov.uk/
United Kingdom Department of Education and Skills

http://www.census.gov/
US Census Bureau

http://www.ed.gov
US Department of Education

Figure 3.2 Sample of useful websites for educational researchers

student records in print or in databases for test scores, grade-point averages, graduation rates, or other achievement data. Because a number of options exist, a researcher must plan ahead, organize, and then select or design an appropriate tool for collecting data. In the following sections, several of the more popular data-collection tools are presented. The tools will also be discussed in later chapters devoted to treatments of the various research methodologies.

Direct observation

Some research methods, such as ethnography and forms of descriptive study, require observation of activities in a school or other natural setting. The observation may be conducted in person or by videotaping, each of which has its drawbacks and advantages.

In-person observations allow an activity to be scanned extensively for relevant behaviors and context. Observers are trained to take careful notes as they look and listen for subtle comments, clues, and nuances such as facial expressions or inflection and tone of voice. However, many times even the best trained observers might miss something important. Also, other researchers not present must rely entirely on the descriptions and notes provided by the observer to recreate the details of the observation in their own minds. Videotaping requires that a camera and other equipment be set up to record an activity. One benefit of videotaping is that the tape can be observed over and over again. A videotape can also be shared with experts who were not present during the original taping in order to receive their comments and advice. Videotaping, however, usually allows for a set number of camera angles and some behaviors might happen outside or in the far reaches of the viewing field. In addition, while videotaping avoids having a stranger or outsider in the setting, having a camera or other equipment visible might lead some individuals "to play to the camera" and not act as they normally do.

When conducting observations in person, the researcher must decide whether the observer is or is not an active participant (i.e., participant observer) in an activity and prepare accordingly. If the purpose of the observation is to record behaviors as objectively and completely as possible with little or no interaction, then the observer must be trained to keep his or her presence to a minimum. On the other hand, if the observer is to participate and assume a role in an activity, then he or she must be trained to act the role. For example, an observer might assume the role of a team-teacher in a class and so must be trained to be a teacher for the duration of the observation.

Observations, whenever possible, should be conducted over a period of time. One-time observations have questionable value since people act and respond differently depending upon circumstances and situations. Accurate depictions require the observer to see and hear activities on multiple occasions. It is not unusual for observations, particularly those involving an educational activity, to go on for a semester or a year or more.

Structured interviews

Structured interviews are carefully scripted tools for collecting data wherein the researcher meets with and asks questions of an individual(s). The structured interview should be well organized and all questions should be developed in advance and written as part of a script that the researcher or interviewer follows. The interview script should contain identification of who is being interviewed and where the interview is being conducted, short-answer questions (either fill in the blank or multiple choice), and open-ended questions that allow the responder to explain how or why something exists or occurs. Open-ended questions also allow the interviewer to pursue a line of questioning and to follow-up with additional questions when the interviewee has mentioned something interesting or provocative. A good technique for designing a structured interview is to start with broad general questions and move on to more direct specific questions depending upon the responses.

Structured interviews are very effective data-collection tools when the interviewer is adept at questioning, can make an interviewee feel comfortable, and is able to prompt honest responses. By the same token, structured interviews can be problematic if the interviewer is not adept or objective. One major concern is prompting an interviewee to respond in a particular way. This is especially pertinent when interviewing children. Arthur Miller's *The Crucible* depicts an extreme example in which child witnesses were "led on" during the Salem witch trials. In recent years, a number of court cases involving pedophilia have been questioned and some decisions overturned because prosecutors have led impressionable children to give false testimony. Whether the subjects are children or adults, questions should be carefully worded to minimize leading the interviewee. For example, an interview of students concerning school safety might start with one of the following questions: "How do you feel about the safety in your school?" "Do you feel this is a safe school?" or "Do you feel more secure inside or outside your school?" Questions designed to provoke should be minimized. For example: "Have you heard any students talking about guns or knives in this school?" or "Do you know of anyone who has had money or other things stolen in this school?"

Structured interviews take time to conduct properly and, for this reason, the researcher must carefully select the interviewees. Unless there is substantial funding for a research project, a small sample of interviewees will be selected who may or may not represent a larger population. If a larger sample is selected and more than one interviewer is used, then the interviewers need to be trained to be consistent in their line of questioning. A good technique in designing a structured interview is to field-test it several times with a very small group of representative interviewees to determine if there are any problems with the wording of questions or any other aspect of the interview. Structured interviews should also be designed to repeat key or important questions in slightly different forms to determine if the interviewees are consistent in their responses. If the interviewees allow it, making an audio tape of each interview will provide a simple mechanism for reviewing notes and responses.

Surveys

While observations and structured interviews are appropriate data-collection tools for small populations, financially and logistically it is difficult, if not impossible, to use them for studies requiring a large number of subjects. Survey research, on the other hand, is one of the most popular tools for collecting data on large samples. It can be used for a number of different research methodologies including descriptive studies, correlation research, and causal comparative research. Some well-respected experts consider survey research as a unique methodology rather than as a data-collection tool (Wiersma, 2000).

The art of conducting a survey includes the following:

- design the instrument
- pilot test
- select a sample
- distribute the survey
- follow-up
- record the data
- analyze the results.

Designing a survey instrument relates directly to the problem or topic being studied and the target survey population. The design of the survey instrument requires in-depth knowledge of the subject matter so that questions are accurate in content and easily under-standable by the survey respondents. Consideration must be given to the reading levels of target populations especially in studies that involve children whose literacy skills are still developing.

Simplicity of format also is an important aspect of survey design. Likert-type scales which ask respondents to select a response from three to seven options in a consistent format are popular in survey research. Depending on the questions, options might be worded as:

Strongly disagree	Disagree	No opinion	Agree	Strongly agree

or

Never		Rarely	Sometimes	Most of the time	Always

or

Strongly disagree	Somewhat disagree	Disagree	No opinion	Agree	Somewhat agree	Strongly agree

The Likert scale is named after Rensis Likert who did an extensive amount of well-respected survey research on leadership and other aspects of organizational behavior at the University of Michigan.

In summary, suggestions for wording questions on a survey include:

• keep them short and direct
• include only one idea or concept per question
• avoid complex terms and difficult language
• make sure that the content is accurate
• make sure that all grammar is correct
• avoid leading the respondent to certain conclusions.

The above suggestions should be carefully considered since many potential respondents will not answer a survey if it looks overly complex, time-consuming, or contains questions that are intimidating or confusing. Consistency in the question format significantly helps respondents understand how to respond to a survey.

Once a survey instrument has been developed, it should be piloted or field-tested on a small group of representative respondents. The pilot test should be designed to determine if any questions are difficult or confusing to answer. A time study should also be conducted to determine how long it takes to complete the survey since the longer the survey, the lower the response rate. If the pilot test indicates minor or modest changes to the instrument, then these should be done immediately and preparation made to distribute the survey to a larger population. If major changes are required, the instrument should be pilot-tested a second time after these changes have been made.

The survey sample will generally be selected randomly and will be much smaller than the larger population that is the focus of the study. The art of selecting a random sample can be complex but essentially requires that all the subjects in a population have an equal chance of being selected for the sample. One popular way to accomplish this is by assigning each potential subject a number, have a computer sort the numbers randomly, then have the computer select every number at a certain interval (e.g., every fifth, tenth, or hundredth) depending on the desired size of the survey sample. A stratified sample is a type of random sample that attempts to include representative proportions of certain characteristics (e.g., gender, ethnicity, income levels) of the larger population. This may be necessary because sometimes in generating a random sample, a disproportionate percentage of subjects with a particular characteristic (e.g., too many females, too many high-income families) are selected. The stratified sample corrects any disproportion.

In considering how to select a sample, a major decision must be made as to whether the survey will be administered once or several times. A cross-sectional study uses stratified, random sampling techniques if the sample is conducted once. Findings and conclusions are stated as applying to the survey population for that particular time.

In a longitudinal study, the researcher surveys a population over time and the survey is administered several times. The researcher has the option of using a new random sample for each administration of the survey or of opting to follow the original sample over time. In the latter case, the random sample selected for the first administration of the survey is also used for each successive administration. When selecting this option, a determination should be made of the sample's mobility and whether or not address or telephone numbers are likely to change during the period of the study.

Surveys are distributed in several ways. Mailings are the most popular. The costs for mailing are modest, the postal services are reliable, and respondents have a chance to peruse the instrument and determine if they wish to participate. If a survey is short and the sample relatively small, a researcher may opt to use the telephone to contact potential respondents. This will likely be more costly and may require several attempts to contact respondents who are away from their phones. In recent years, survey designers have been using Internet websites to conduct surveys. While this type of survey is relatively inexpensive, its greatest benefit may be that the results are collected in electronic form and are available for immediate analysis. The major drawback is that not everyone is connected to the Internet.

When conducting a survey, a major question is: what is an acceptable response rate? This is difficult to answer and will depend upon the nature of the survey. Many researchers working with stable populations and questions that are not considered overly sensitive will seek high (e.g., in excess of 50 percent) response rates. However, if the survey touches on sensitive issues (e.g., sexual practices, drug use) or the population is highly mobile (e.g., student drop-outs) then lower response rates are to be expected. If there is any question about the response rate, a second or third follow-up distribution of the survey is appropriate.

If survey data have been collected using print or the telephone, the results will need to be recorded and stored in an electronic (computer) form, assuming that the data will be analyzed, sorted, and reviewed using computer software tools rather than manually. Depending on the size of the sample, this can be a time-consuming task and also error-prone if not done properly. Large research organizations usually employ professional data-entry clerks to record survey results. To minimize errors, a well-designed survey will take into consideration how the results will be recorded so that coding schemes will be simple and straightforward. A coding scheme refers to the final valid possibilities that can occur for an item on a survey. For instance, gender might appear on the survey as a check-off box that indicates "Female" or "Male." However, when the response to this question is recorded electronically, it may appear as a code such as "1" or "2," or "F" or "M." The coding of a survey may or may not be done by someone intimately familiar with the study and so the simpler the code, the fewer the errors. For most statistical analyses, a coding scheme that converts item responses into numbers rather than letters of the alphabet is highly recommended.

Once the data are converted into electronic form, they are ready to be analyzed. The nature of survey analysis requires that a computer software program be used to sort and perform the appropriate statistical routines on the data. At this point, the researcher may wish to work with someone who is knowledgable about the topic to help review the results. Reading and reviewing the results of statistical analyses can be a lonely and at times frustrating activity, and it helps to have someone to share the burden.

Test instruments

Test instruments are used to collect data for certain educational research topics and problems. For instance, student achievement is an area of study that frequently requires testing. While some researchers will consider developing their own test instruments, this is not the recommended approach. Over the past 40 years, many excellent test instruments on a wide variety of topics have been developed. Deciding which of these instruments is appropriate for a research topic should be the first choice of individual researchers.

Test instruments are available from commercial vendors, colleges and universities, and test organizations. *Tests in Print* is probably the best source for locating an appropriate test instrument. This multi-volume reference is published by the Buros Institute of Mental Measurements, and updated every three or four years, and contains reviews of thousands of test instruments. Another popular source is the ERIC/ETS Test Locator website which is available online at <http://ericae.net/testcol.htm>. This database contains thousands of descriptions of test instruments and publishers. It is updated regularly by the Educational Testing Service (ETS). The source material for this website is the *ETS Collection of Tests* which is available in multi-volume print form as well as on microfiche.

In reviewing the appropriateness of a test instrument, a researcher should pay particular attention to the information provided on reliability and validity. Correlation coefficients are used extensively to measure the reliability (consistency of results) and validity (measures what it is supposed to measure) of standardized tests.

Determining reliability usually involves giving the same test to the same sample of subjects two or more times and then comparing results using correlations which one would expect to be very high. In another approach, the same sample of subjects take a different set of questions of the same test at two different times and compare results using correlation coefficients. For example, the sample may take the odd-numbered questions on a Monday and then take the even-numbered questions on a Thursday. A correlational analysis is then performed on the results of the two days of testing.

Validity tests can be performed by correlating the results of one test with a similar measure that has already established its validity.

For example, validity tests for making predictions such as the use of Scholastic Aptitude Test (SAT) scores to predict college grade-point average, might use correlation coefficients of the two measures (SAT scores and grade-point averages) of a sample population to establish the predictive validity of the SAT. In cases where an appropriate measure to compare results of a test is not available, validity tests for content of subject matter frequently have to be done by a panel of experts who attest to the validity of the test. In establishing reliability and validity of standardized tests, very high correlations (e.g., +.80 and above) are expected.

If a researcher decides that an appropriate test instrument is not available, designing a new test becomes a major undertaking. The process is similar to designing a survey but will require rigorous pilot or field-testing on multiple subject samples. Reliability and validity analysis is also expected which can be costly in terms of both time and finances.

Using multiple data-collection tools
While not all research is conducive to a combination approach, certain topics or methodologies, especially descriptive research, provide opportunities for researchers to combine two or more tools. For instance, research on technology use in schools may be done through surveys sent to a large sample of school principals. After the surveys have been collected and the initial data analyzed, structured interviews of a smaller sample of principals may be used to follow-up on certain aspects of the survey results which might need clarification, such as teacher training or curriculum development. In this example, the structured interviews are used to enhance the survey results and to provide a more complete description or picture. With so much debate in educational research circles regarding qualitative versus quantitative approaches, a combined approach might take advantage of the best aspects of the two.

TOOLS FOR ANALYSIS

To some, the most interesting aspect of a research project is analyzing the data. For qualitative data, much of the analysis will depend upon carefully reviewing field notes, viewing videotapes, or listening to audiotapes. The data from these sources need to be categorized according to their origin, concepts, and themes. The researcher also needs to establish some system of organization conducive to developing a coding scheme that will allow quick access to common items. A computerized database system might be most helpful in this regard because it allows the researcher to establish a keyword system to find and locate common codes, entries, and phrases. Generally a record is made of each observation or structured interview and keywords, codes, or phrases are established along with a concise record of the field notes. All modern database systems provide a query language that allows the user to access keywords and identifiers that exist in each record. Researchers not familiar with database software should take a workshop on one of the popular database packages, such as Microsoft's Access, or otherwise seek assistance in setting up a database. It should be noted that a database does not do analysis but makes it easier for the researcher to access the data for analysis. In addition to generic database software programs, there are custom database programs designed to handle qualitative data. *The Ethnograph* (Qualis Research Associates, Salt Lake City, Utah, <http://www.QualisResearch.com>) is a versatile computer program designed to make the analysis of data collected during qualitative research easier, more efficient, and more effective. Developed in 1985, *The Ethnograph* has pioneered computer-assisted qualitative data analysis. *The Ethnograph* handles project data files and documents in the form of interview transcripts, field notes, open-ended survey responses, and other text-based documents. *The Ethnograph* helps to search and note segments of interest within qualitative data files, mark them with code words, and run analyses which can be retrieved for inclusion in reports or for further analysis. QSR International Pty Ltd. (Melbourne, Australia, <http//www.qsr.com.au>) offers several software packages which assist researchers in organizing and analyzing complex qualitative data. *N6*, the latest version of its *NUD*IST* (*Non-numerical Unstructured Data; Indexing, Searching, and Theorizing*) software, and *NVivo* allow the researcher to import and code textual data, edit the text without affecting the coding; retrieve, review, and recode coded data; search for combinations of words in the text or patterns in coding; and import data from and export data to quantitative analysis software.

For quantitative data analysis, researchers will also likely use a computer software package. The day of using a hand calculator to do statistical analysis is long gone and every serious researcher needs to familiarize him or herself with a modern statistical software tool. Before using a statistical software tool, all data must be coded and converted into an electronic form. Electronic spreadsheet software programs such as Microsoft's EXCEL are at the low end of statistical tools. They are fine for simple descriptive analyses such as frequency distributions and means. However, for more sophisticated analysis, more powerful tools such as the Statistical Package for the Social Sciences (SPSS), the Statistical Analysis System (SAS), or the Biomedical Data Package (BMDP) are recommended. They provide all the facilities of an electronic spreadsheet program plus graceful routines for doing more complex statistical routines such as t test, analysis of variance, and correlations. In addition, because they were designed for statistical research, these software tools usually provide excellent documentation on using the routines as well as guides for interpreting results. Many a graduate student has learned a good deal of statistics by reading the software documentation provided by SPSS or SAS. If a researcher is not familiar with these packages, a workshop or course may be well worth the time and effort. Without developing this expertise, a researcher will rely on the expertise of others to analyze any substantial amount of quantitative data. Those who have done data analysis using statistical packages know that the more comfortable one is with working and "mining" the data, the more complete the analysis will be. In this primer, SPSS will be used to provide examples of statistical routines.

Qualitative methods: ethnography, historical research, and case studies

Margaret Mead is among the best-known cultural anthropologists of the twentieth century. She wrote 44 books and more than 1000 articles on topics that included child rearing, adolescent behavior, and learning theory. She was the curator of ethnology at the American Museum of Natural History and president of the American Science Society. Her pioneering work was in ethnographic research where she stressed the importance of detailed observation in natural settings. She was amongst the earliest ethnographers to use still photography and later film to document what she saw in the field. Her first major book, *Coming of Age in Samoa* (1928), is considered a classic ethnographic study, and reports on two years' worth of research during which she lived, worked, and played with Pacific Islanders in their villages.

Her work, while highly respected worldwide, has come under intense scrutiny by the academic community. Derek Freeman, a professor at the Research School of Pacific and Asian Studies in the Institute of Advanced Studies at the Australian National University, made a lifelong study of the people of Samoa and followed-up on much of Mead's work there. In 1983, a few years after her death, Freeman published *Margaret Mead and Samoa*, a book that was highly critical of Mead's research methods. He claimed that her work was flawed and influenced far too much by her own biases. He objected to her use of superlatives such as "always" and "never" in reporting her observations. Freeman's book precipitated a debate on Mead and her research. Ray McDermott, a professor of education and anthropology at Stanford University, commented on the work of Mead and Freeman in Samoa as:

> Where Mead saw free love, Freeman counted rape; where Mead saw generosity and detachment, Freeman found jealousy

and aggression; where Mead saw cooperation, Freeman found hierarchy and ambivalence. (McDermott, 2001, p. 849)

Despite the controversy, Mead's research has influenced and will continue to influence how people think about gender and sexuality, adolescent development, and children and learning. Freeman's criticism likewise continues to be of interest to anthropologists and others.

QUALITATIVE RESEARCH

The topic of this chapter is qualitative methods, specifically ethnography, historical research, and case studies. The story of Margaret Mead serves as an appropriate introduction because she championed its techniques. Quality refers to the essence (what, why, when, and how) of things while quantity refers to the amount of something. Qualitative research relies on the meanings, concepts, context, descriptions, and settings while quantitative research relies on measurements and counts (Berg, 2004). Both approaches stress the importance of objectivity in observations and data collection, although qualitative research by its very nature is more dependent upon a researcher's subjective interpretation. Qualitative research requires seeing and hearing and, perhaps, touching and experiencing activities in natural environments. Quantitative research requires a distancing from the object of study and that the sorting, counting, and analysis of numerical data be done away from their sources. A grand debate has existed for decades on the virtues of one approach over the other. Rather than enter this debate, we note that both approaches are highly respected and, when done well, add equally to the knowledge base. Where possible, researchers should consider using the techniques of both approaches to conduct their studies thereby validating results through more than one perspective.

ETHNOGRAPHY

The nature of ethnographic research
Ethnography stems from the Greek "ethnos" meaning people, tribes, or nations and "graphy" meaning writing. Ethnographic research is the writing about people in their natural or social setting. It is a form of descriptive research and is also referred to as "observational research" and "naturalistic inquiry." As a part of

the social sciences, it has been especially popular in cultural anthropology research because of the work of Margaret Mead and other noted anthropologists. Ethnography is well-suited to research in education as well because so much of what is done in education is based on human interaction in natural and social settings such as schools, classrooms, and playgrounds.

Good ethnographic research requires training and discipline: training in observation and discipline in suppressing subjectivity and recording observations objectively. The latter is difficult to achieve because most of us do not fully understand our own biases and prejudices in observing others. In addition to the question of subjectivity, a major drawback of ethnography is that the researcher cannot infer from a small sample to larger populations. Any inferences made in an ethnographic study are there for the readers to accept or reject. On the other hand, a major benefit of ethnographic research is that it provides rich descriptions of human behavior in natural settings and not in artificially constructed experimental settings.

The observation of a phenomenon in its natural or social setting may appear on the surface to be very straightforward. In this regard, Yvonna Lincoln, an expert in the use of qualitative research methods, refers to the work of Alfred Schultz who formulated a theory of multiple realities. This theory essentially proposes that what we see is shaped by our own value systems and that the same phenomenon might be "seen" and interpreted differently depending upon our background, experiences, and values. In terms of naturalistic research:

> participants ... create realities ... that are based on multiple and often conflicting value systems. Evaluators must take each construction into account and recognize that no single reality exists.... (Lincoln, 1986, p. 1)

If this is so, ethnographic researchers need to understand the lens through which they see the world and provide for other interpretations. This can be accomplished in several ways depending upon the topic being studied:

1. Have observations performed by more than one observer.
2. Use videotape to record observations and ask others (experienced observers) to validate the prime observer's findings.
3. Use multiple tools for data collection such as observations, interviews, and questionnaires.

These will be discussed in more detail later on in this chapter.

Process and procedures in ethnography
The first step in planning any project is identifying a topic worthy of study. For ethnography, the topic selected should require or benefit from studying a phenomenon in a natural setting. This also implies that the researcher has access to the natural setting. In education, topics suitable for an ethnographic study include:

- instructional interaction of teachers in classrooms
- social interactions of students in a classroom, library or playground
- the behavior of a principal in implementing an initiative, reform, or curricular approach
- group counseling processes such as the assignment of special education services.

Once a topic has been selected, the researcher needs to identify the person(s) who can provide the requisite permission for conducting observations in the natural setting (school, classroom, playground, library).

Hypotheses and research questions (see Figure 4.1) in ethnographic research are stated very broadly at the onset of the study and can be further developed as data are collected and analyzed. In some exploratory ethnographic studies, it may not be necessary to state a hypothesis or research question initially; it might be preferable to wait and see how the observations evolve and develop. Such studies may simply have general statements of purpose such as:

This study will examine race relations in an urban school.
This study will examine decision-making at the_____
Board of Education.
This study will examine gender relations in a computer science laboratory.

In ethnography, whether or not hypotheses or research questions are stated initially is entirely at the discretion of the researcher.

The next step in the ethnographic study process is to establish a schedule of visits to the natural setting to conduct observations and/or videotaping. If possible, more than one observer should be used to broaden interpretations of the setting, the phenomenon, and social interactions. All parties need to know the schedule and be prepared for the visit. To the extent possible, the researcher

Purpose	To describe and interpret a phenomenon that has been observed in its natural setting.
Hypothesis/Research questions	Stated broadly at the beginning of the study and evolves as data are collected and analyzed.
Data collection/Sources	Observations, photography, and videotaping of events in the natural setting. Field notes provide the major research record which will be used for analysis.
Data analysis	Field notes are converted into electronic form and analyzed using software such as databases, query programs, and other computer software packages. These tools are used to support the researcher's intuition and interpretation of the observed phenomenon.
Reporting results	Rich descriptions of the setting, subjects, and phenomenon observed. Rationale that formed the basis of the interpretation of the data is also presented.

Figure 4.1 Planning for ethnographic research

should interfere minimally with the phenomenon being observed. Field notes comprise the major data-collection activity. These notes should be detailed, well-organized, and coded and converted into electronic (computer) form as quickly as possible. Any questions or issues that need follow-up should also be done as soon as possible after an observation(s). Additional observations and interviews may be necessary to help clarify any questions. Videotaping is extremely helpful in this regard because it can be viewed over and over again. Also it can easily be shared with someone who might have particular expertise or knowledge of the activity.

Triangulation is an important technique that is used in many forms of qualitative research. It is especially useful in ethnographies to address the limitations of a single data source. Triangulation takes many forms but essentially it is a multi-pronged approach to data collection. Two or more data-collection techniques (documents and interviews; observations and documents; documents, observations, and interviews) are used to collect data on the same item of analysis. For instance, in order to collect data on a school's spirit, an ethnographer might: look at documents such as school newspapers; examine student records to determine participation in extra-curricular activities; observe behaviors of teachers in social settings such as the teachers' lounge; and interview students. Where there is convergence or consistency among the different data-collection techniques, the ethnographer can be secure in pursuing or reporting a particular finding. Where there is not convergence or consistency, the ethnographer can either develop further data-collection techniques to seek corroboration or abandon a particular finding or interpretation.

Data analysis consists of a careful review of the researcher's field notes, videotape, interview notes, and other documentation collected during the observations. Converting this material into electronic form and using a software program such as *The Ethnograph* or a generic database software package will make searching and sorting data much easier. Because much of ethnographic research depends upon the observer's interpretation of the phenomenon, sharing initial findings with someone who is familiar with the topic, the subjects, or the setting is most helpful and will validate the observer's interpretation.

In keeping with the purpose of ethnographic research, a rich description of the setting is an absolute necessity. In presenting results and writing a report, the reader should be able to feel, see, and experience the setting. Subjects should be described in detail so that an image can easily be formed in the reader's mind. If photography was used, pictures can be included in the report assuming that the proper permissions have been obtained. The researcher should also discuss the rationales in interpreting the data collected during the observations. Ethnographic reports are generally lengthy because of the need for the rich descriptions of the setting, people, and groups involved. As a result, many ethnographic studies evolve into book-length treatments.

Figure 4.2 is an excerpt from the methodology section of an ethnographic study that followed two meetings of the Committee on Special Education in a public school in a small town in upstate New York for one adolescent girl. The details of the observations, the time devoted to the study, and the variety of ethnographic techniques used to collect data are presented. Readers who wish to pursue further information on ethnography may search ERIC or Wilson Web (Education) Full Text Services, and use the keyword "ethnography."

This excerpt is taken from an article entitled, "Through the eyes of the institution: A critical discourse analysis of decision making in two special education meetings" by Rebecca Rogers. It was published in *Anthropology & Education Quarterly* **33**(2): 213–37, June 2002. The entire article is available on the Internet from Wilson Web (Education) Full Text Services.

The data used for this analysis were drawn from a two-year **ethnographic study** of literacy and language practices in the community of Sherman Hollows. ... Data collection occurred from September of 1997 to September of 1999. Over the two years of the study, I worked as a participant-observer in the Treaders' home and community of Sherman Hollows.

In investigating each of these contexts, I used ethnographic methods of participant-observation (Spradley 1980), in-depth and life history interviews (Rubin and Rubin 1995), semistructured interviews, document collection, photography (Hamilton 2000), and archival research (e.g., census data, historical records). The primary data sources included over 300 hundred hours of audiotaped interactions in the Treaders' home, community, and school. I also interviewed members in both the school and the community of Sherman Hollows. This included June's adult basic education teacher and Vicky's classroom (sixth and seventh grade) and remedial reading teachers. I conducted interviews with members of the Treaders' social network that included the alderman, the priests and ministers of several churches, the leader of a community-organizing agency, the president of the parent-teacher association, a barber, and a worker at a community coalition. I attended community-organizing meetings. Secondary data sources included participants' journals, informal surveys, and documents collected from various events.

My observations included over 500 hours of participant-observation in the Treaders' home and community. During this time I handwrote field notes that were then entered into a database after leaving the site. Similarly, I observed twice a month during the 1997–98 school year in Vicky's and June's **classrooms**. In the community, I was a participant-observer in several organizations and gatherings, including a community speak-out, a meeting held about gang violence, a meeting concerning partnering the school with other community agencies, a PTA meeting at the school, district budget meetings, church, barbecues, and community picnics.

Figure 4.2 Sample methodology from an ethnographic study

HISTORICAL RESEARCH

The nature of historical research

Historical research, also referred to as historiography, is a form of descriptive research. It involves describing and interpreting events, conditions, or situations that have occurred in the past in order to understand the present, and perhaps to plan for the future. A common characteristic of historical research is an in-depth analysis of source documents (e.g., student transcripts, policy statements, memoranda) and oral histories, if individuals or recordings are available from the period. In terms of the number of studies conducted on an annual basis, it is possibly the least popular form of educational research since foundations, government agencies, and other funding organizations tend to favor current issues and conditions. Furthermore, historical research can be difficult if the period being studied is remote to the extent that records are not readily available and individuals associated with the period or event are no longer alive. However, historical research can be a most interesting activity as the researcher attempts to recreate or uncover a "story" from long ago. Its value increases significantly if a connection can be made to a present issue or situation.

Most historical research relies on qualitative research methods, however, if quantitative data such as grade reports, test scores, or census data are available, the researcher should consider using them to support the qualitative analysis. As electronic archives expand, more reliable quantitative data are becoming available for historical research purposes.

Process and procedures in historical research
The first step in planning a historical study is identifying a topic rooted in the past that is of interest to the researcher. In education, topics suitable for a historical study include:

- a school that typified a community or era
- a policy or legal issue
- a social history of community involvement in education
- an event that had a significant influence on education.

Critical to the choices is the availability of data from the period. If data are available, a careful analysis has to be made as to their authenticity and completeness, and the cost (time and money) for accessing them.

Hypothesis and research questions (see Figure 4.3) in historical research are broadly stated. Researchers also may use the statement of purpose to imply a hypothesis or research question. Examples of hypotheses and research questions suitable for use in historical research include:

How desegregation after the US Supreme Court Decision Brown v. Board of Education (1954) changed a public school in _____.

The union movement in the 1960s improved the employment conditions for teachers in _____.

How did school decentralization effect the governance of public schools in New York City in the 1970s?

In historical research, a good deal of leeway is allowed in the formulation of hypotheses or research questions. As with ethnography, the historical researcher can use his or her discretion.

The critical task in planning a historical research project is identifying accessible data sources (e.g., official documents, reports, and oral histories). The more distant in the past is the topic of research, the more difficult it will be to locate data. Historical researchers must be scrupulous in establishing the authenticity and reliability of data sources. Official documents may exist in a school archive, however, the researcher needs to determine whether the records are complete or if anything critical is missing or has been destroyed.

Purpose	To describe and interpret events, conditions, or situations of the past.
Hypothesis/Research questions	Stated broadly at the beginning of the study or implied in the statement of purpose.
Data collection/ Sources	Structured interviews, oral histories, relics, primary documents such as official school records, student transcripts, and memoranda. Quantitative data such as grade reports if available can also be collected.
Data analysis	Responses and notes are converted into electronic form and analyzed using software such as databases, query programs, and other computer software packages. These tools are used to support the researcher's intuition and interpretation of the data. Any quantitative data can be analyzed using a computer software program, such as SPSS, to conduct simple descriptive analysis (e.g., frequency distributions, means, standard deviations).
Reporting results	Rich descriptions of the setting, subjects, and the event, condition, or situation. Attempt to connect the past event, condition, or situation to the present-day.

Figure 4.3 Planning for historical research

In historical research, *external criticism* and *internal criticism* establish the authenticity and usefulness of a document. External criticism establishes genuineness and provides some proof that a document is what it purports to be. Official seals on school records and corroboration of a report through a reliable secondary witness are examples of how the authenticity can be established. Internal criticism establishes that the content of a document is useful. In examining a historical document, the researcher has to look at questions such as: "Did the author of the document really have reliable information?", "Was the author biased in any way?", or "Was the author mislead by someone in recording an event?" These determinations can be especially difficult in cases where authors of documents have a close relationship to an event or issue. For example, a principal of a school may record incidents or events from a point of view presenting his or her school in the best light. Since the researcher cannot rely on a single historical document, cross-referencing one source with others establishes authenticity and usefulness. The use of triangulation as discussed earlier in this chapter is appropriate for historical research.

Historical information may be gathered and preserved through oral history. If the researcher can locate individuals who observed, participated in, or are otherwise knowledgable about a past event, tape-recording an interview with them can yield valuable information. An oral history interview should be structured with pre-established questions. However, it should also allow the interviewee the flexibility to expand and explore his or her thoughts. Oral history is an excellent technique for corroborating written data sources such as documents and reports. The researcher needs to be aware of nostalgic fondness for a bygone era and selective memory about the past. Increasingly, many research and civic groups are collecting oral histories and making them available in digital archives. On undertaking a historical study, a researcher might want to search these archives, many of which are available on the Internet. Figure 4.4 is a list of websites that provide information on digital archives of oral history materials.

Data analysis requires a careful review of the researcher's notes, audio tape of oral histories, interview notes, and any other documentation that might have been collected. As much data as possible should be converted into electronic form. If quantitative data were collected, they should be coded and prepared for descriptive statistical analysis. Sharing initial findings with someone who is

British Library
http://www.bl.uk

British Library Sound Archive
http://www.bl.uk/collections/sound-archive/history.html

Canadian Oral History Association
http://www.ncf.carleton.ca/oral-history

International Oral History Association
http://www.ioha.fgv.br

Mass-Observation Archive, University of Sussex
http://www.sussex.ac.uk/library/massobs/homearch.html

Michigan Oral History Association
http://www.ok-history.mus.ok.us/folk/flc1.html

National Library of Australia Oral History Collection
http://www.nla.gov.au/oh

National Library of New Zealand Oral History Centre
http://www.natlib.govt.nz/public/virtual_tour/oral_history.htm

Oral History Association (US)
http://omega.dickinson.edu/organizations/oha

Oral History Collection, Oklahoma Historical Society
http://www.h-net.msu.edu/~moha

Oral History Research Office Columbia University, New York
http://www.columbia.edu/cu/libraries/indiv/oral

Oral History Society (UK)
http://www.oralhistory.org.uk

School of Scottish Studies, University of Edinburgh
http://www.sss.ed.ac.uk

Smithsonian Institution Archives
http://www.siris.si.edu

Southern Oral History Program, University of North Carolina at Chapel Hill
http://www.unc.edu/depts/sohp

University of California at Los Angeles (UCLA) Oral History Program
http://www2.library.ucla.edu/libraries/special/ohp/ohpindex.htm

University of New South Wales Oral History Program, Sydney, Australia
http://www.oralhistory.unsw.edu.au

US Library of Congress WPA Federal Writers' Project Life Stories
http://lcweb2.loc.gov/ammem/wpaintro/wpahome.html

Figure 4.4 Oral history websites

familiar with the topic will help validate the researcher's interpretation.

In presenting results and writing a report, a rich description of the setting and subjects is common. The reader should be able to travel back in time and have a sense of what it would have been like in the setting. In presenting findings and results, the researcher should also provide the rationales for interpreting the data collected during the observations. If quantitative data were collected, they should be presented using descriptive statistics such as frequency distributions, contingency tables, and means. Despite the possible difficulties, an attempt should be made to connect the topic to the present. This can add significantly to the importance of the historical study.

Historical reports can be lengthy because of the need for rich descriptions of the setting, people, and groups involved. Book-length treatments are common.

Figure 4.5 is an excerpt from the methodology section of a historical study that followed the development of the Caswell County Training School (CCTS) in rural North Carolina during the period of 1933–69. Prior to the Brown v. Board of Education (1954) decision, CCTS was a segregated school attended by African–American children. The author, Vanessa Siddle Walker, looked at the relationship of the African–American community to CCTS prior to and after integration. The techniques used to minimize any bias in data collection are noted. Ms. Walker won a number of awards for her research including the 1998 Early Career Award from the American Educational Research Association. A shorter version of this study is available under the title, "Caswell County Training School, 1933–1969: Relationship between community and school," (*Harvard Education Review*, **63**(2): 161–82), Summer 1993. Readers who wish to pursue further information on historical research should do a search of ERIC or Wilson Web (Education) Full Text Services, and use keyword "historiography."

CASE–STUDY METHODOLOGY

The nature of case study

Case-study research is descriptive research that involves describing and interpreting events, conditions, or situations that are occurring in the present. The purpose of a case study is to examine in detail a specific activity, event, organization, or person(s). The choice of object in a case-study analysis is at the discretion of the researcher

This excerpt is taken from a book entitled *Their Highest Potential: An African–American School Community in the Segregated South* by Vanessa Siddle Walker. It was published by the University of North Carolina Press (1996). The study examined the Caswell County Training School (North Carolina) during the period of 1933–69.

The themes discussed ... emerged from six years of collecting data that included both documents and interviews. In general because CCTS [Caswell County Training School] school files – with the exception of one thin folder – were discarded at the onset of desegregation, primary documents relating to the school were almost uniformly located in the homes of members of the local African–American community. In some cases ... primary documents [e.g., principal reports, local newspaper accounts, and school board meetings] relating to the school were housed in archival collections....

With four exceptions, informants selected for interviews held one of four relationships with the school – parent, student, teacher, administrator....

One of the most serious threats to the reconstruction of this story has been the influence of nostalgia, or "euphoria recall" as Robert Thompson has labeled the pervasive tendency of people to recall with fondness the "goodness" of a previous time in their lives. Because of the heavy reliance on interviews in the telling of the story, the methodology specifically attempted to minimize the romanticization that reasonably could occur in retrospective recountings. The most dominant method employed was the triangulation of documentation with interviews. ... Interviews were used to reconstruct the thematic points of emphasis described in the story, documents were important means of confirming and expanding the themes.

A second threat to the interpretation of the data is my relationship* to the community and the school, and thus my possible bias. On one hand, the relationship was an advantage. I am unsure I could have achieved access as quickly without the entree provided by my background. ... Given that most of the most important documentation "finds" were located in people's homes. On the other hand, my closeness to the community could also cause me to miss the significance or subtle meaning or to be skewed in my interpretation of events. To limit these biases ... two research assistants (one who had no familiarity with the area or the era and one who knew the area but had not attended the school) applied additional lenses on the interpretation of the data.

[*Note: The researcher was a student at CCTS, her mother was a teacher, and her father was a PTA president.]

Figure 4.5 Sample methodology from a historical study

and can be, for example, a single school district, a school, a class, a group of students, or an individual student. The last of these examples is, by the way, very common in special education where teachers work one-on-one with students. Case study is a very flexible methodology that comes in many different forms including descriptive, exploratory, longitudinal, and multi-site. Other professions namely medicine, law, criminology, and social work use case-study methodology extensively.

Among the various educational research methodologies, case study is one of the most popular used by individual researchers, especially graduate students. Many graduate students are familiar with its techniques because a number of graduate programs have developed components of their curricula which use case-study analysis. Students are asked to assume roles within a case study in which they pursue an issue or decision, or handle a situation. The Harvard School of Education, for instance, is well known for its collection of case studies used in its academic programs.

While most case studies rely on qualitative approaches, quantitative techniques are common as well. Many case studies combine the two, initially using qualitative approaches that rely on interviews and reviews of documents, and then following-up with an analysis using quantitative data gathered via surveys, questionnaires, or school databases.

As with other qualitative methodologies, such as ethnography and historiography, the researcher using case-study methodology must be careful about his or her objectivity in interviewing or observing subjects. Also, since case study concentrates on a single specific activity or entity, the researcher cannot generalize the study's findings to larger populations. Any inferences are left to the reader of the case study.

Process and procedures in case-study methodology
The first step in planning a case study is identifying a current topic that is of interest to the researcher. In education, topics suitable for a case study are extensive and might include:

- a decision of a board of education
- the implementation of a new policy, curriculum reform, or process in a school
- a staff development activity
- a class project
- an individual child's progress over the school year.

Almost any person, place, or thing in education is a potential topic for case-study research.

Hypotheses and research questions (see Figure 4.6) in case

studies are broadly stated. Examples of hypotheses and research questions suitable for use in case study research include:

Technology improves student writing performance in a sixth grade class in Public School_____.
The implementation of school-based management improved staff morale in_____High School.
How did the implementation of the Reading Recovery Program affect student performance in Public School_____?

As with other qualitative methods, the researcher has a good deal of freedom in developing hypotheses and research questions.

Data for case studies can come from many different sources including observation, interviews, documentation, student records, and school databases. Typically the researcher collects a good deal of data and then spends time sorting it out for common themes. The

Purpose	To describe and interpret events, conditions, or situations of the present. A case study concentrates on a detailed examination of a specific activity, event, school or other educational organization, or person(s).
Hypothesis/Research questions	Stated broadly at the beginning of the study.
Data collection/ Sources	Structured interviews, primary documents such as official school records, student transcripts, and memoranda. Quantitative data from surveys, questionnaires, and school databases.
Data analysis	Interview responses and notes are converted into electronic form and analyzed using software such as databases, query programs, and other computer software packages. These tools are used to support the researcher's intuition and interpretation of the data. Any quantitative data can be analyzed using a computer software program such as SPSS to conduct simple descriptive analysis (e.g., frequency distributions, means, standard deviations).
Reporting results	Rich descriptions of the setting, subjects, and the event, condition, or situation. Use quantitative data to back-up interpretations and findings. Since the case study concentrates on a specific activity or entity, the researcher should be careful in trying to infer that the findings can be generalized to larger populations.

Figure 4.6 Planning for case-study research

researcher must obtain permission from appropriate authorities especially if students will be involved. A good research plan includes multiple strategies for collecting data on a single item of analysis. Techniques and concepts such as triangulation, extrinsic criticism, and intrinsic criticism discussed earlier in this chapter are appropriate here as well. Because so many school systems have come to rely on computerized record-keeping systems, the researcher should consider requesting use of these databases and other quantitative data to validate findings.

As mentioned earlier, case-study research can take several forms. Berg (2004) identifies eleven different forms. A case study can be used to explore, to describe, or to explain a phenomenon. Phenomena can be examined at a particular moment (take a snapshot), over time (longitudinally), at a single place, or at multiple sites. The inherent flexibility of the case study adds to its popularity and hence has become a methodology of choice among many individual researchers.

The case-study researcher has an extensive array of data-collection tools available. Any qualitative data-collection tool (e.g., observation, structured interviews, document analysis) can be used in a case study. Field notes, audiotape recordings, and videotape can be used to record observations and subjects. In addition, quantitative data gathered from surveys, questionnaires, grade reports, and school databases can also be used.

Data analysis requires a careful review of the researcher's field notes taken during observations or interviews, audio or videotape, and any other documentation that might have been collected. As much of this data as possible should be converted into electronic form. If quantitative data were collected, they should be coded and prepared for descriptive statistical analysis. Sharing initial findings with someone who is familiar with the topic will help validate the researcher's interpretation.

A description of the setting and subjects is commonly included in the research report. In presenting findings and results, the researcher should provide the rationales used in interpreting the data collected during the observations. If quantitative data were collected, they should be presented using descriptive statistics such as frequency distributions, contingency tables, and means. Since the case study concentrates on a specific activity or entity, the researcher should be careful not to infer that the findings can be generalized to other populations. This is best left to the judgment of the reader.

Figures 4.7 and 4.8 are excerpts from two case-study research projects. The excerpts are provided to show the flexibility of the case-study approach. In Figure 4.7, the excerpt is from a case study entitled "Case studies of families doing third-grade homework" by Jianzhong Xu and Lyn Corno, which examines the homework activities of six children enrolled in the third grade of one public school in New York City. Figure 4.8 is an excerpt from a multi-site case study entitled, "Rethinking 'High Stakes': lessons from the United States and England and Wales," by William Firestone and David Mayrowetz, which looks at the effects of standardized testing

---

This excerpt is taken from an article entitled "Case studies of families doing third-grade homework" by Jianzhong Xu and Lyn Corno. It was published in the *Teachers College Record*, **100**(2): 402–36, Winter 1998. The entire article is available on the Internet from Wilson Web (Education) Full Text Services.

Case study methodology was used to highlight the research questions concerning "how" and "why" particular events occurred. ... Case studies also permitted in-depth analysis of individual families while remaining comprehensive enough to sample a range of interaction patterns across families....

Participants were six third-grade children from one K-5 public school in New York City and their parents, who volunteered. ... We contacted the Parent-Teacher Association and the principal to get permission to put a notice in the school's weekly newsletter seeking volunteers. Eight parents volunteered initially. However, two original volunteers withdrew prior to data collection, each citing discomfort with in-home videotaping....

Data were collected through three sources: (1) open-ended interviews with children, their parents, and teachers; (2) videotapes of two homework sessions in each family; and (3) stimulated-recall interviews with parents following each homework session. ... During the study all families were visited at least five times, with each visit lasting an average of three hours. Data were collected in the form of field notes as well as audiotapes and videotapes....

DATA ANALYSIS
Multiple sources of evidence and triangulation were employed. Patton (1980) and Yin (1984) suggest this tactic as a means of enhancing internal validity and safeguarding against researcher bias. Thus a converging line of inquiry was developed. For example, data from one source (e.g., interview) and perspective (e.g., a parent) were compared with data from another source (e.g., observation) or perspective (e.g., child) with the intention of verifying, clarifying, and amplifying the meaning of findings taken from any single source or perspective. This method also enhanced reliability claims for each individual data source (Guba and Lincoln, 1982); Yin (1984) and consequently, of the overall study.

Figure 4.7 Sample methodology from a case study I

This excerpt is taken from an article entitled, "Rethinking 'High Stakes': Lessons from the United States and England and Wales" by William Firestone and David Mayrowetz. It was published in the *Teachers College Record*, **102**(4): 724–49, August 2000. The entire article is available on the Internet from Wilson Web (Education) Full Text Services.

... [The] research projects used embedded case studies to clarify how assessment policies were interpreted. Conducted in 1995–1996, the American study focused on four schools in two districts in Maryland and eight schools in three Maine districts....

In each district, semi-structured interviews were conducted with school board members, the superintendent, district curriculum specialists, principals, department heads in math, English, and social studies. In addition, 25 mathematics teachers across the two states were visited on two occasions to interviews and observed....

The European fieldwork – conducted in Bristol and Cardiff in the spring of 1997 – was designed to parallel the American procedures as much as possible. A middle income and a low income school was chosen in each city. Interviews were conducted with head teachers (the equivalent of American principals), the senior management team responsible for curriculum, and mathematics department heads. In addition, two visits to 16 teachers were made for classroom observations and interviews. ... The interview guides used in England and Wales drew from those used in Maine and Maryland but were shortened somewhat and modified to reflect the different national context....

Data were entered into NUD*IST, a computerized data analysis package, and coded using a system that began from initial hypotheses but was elaborated inductively through a review of interviews and observation notes. The coding scheme permitted identifying themes and developing and testing larger arguments as suggested by Strauss and Corbin (1990). The American data were analyzed first, and provided some directions for comparing American and English–Welsh data.

Figure 4.8 Sample methodology from a case study II

on twelve schools in the United States and two schools in the United Kingdom. While both studies vary significantly in scope (from six students in one grade in one school in one city to thousands of students in fourteen schools in two countries), the case-study methodologies are similar. In addition, Figure 4.7 includes a description of the use of videotape and other techniques to reduce bias. In Figure 4.8, the authors state that they had to make adjustments for the case studies in England and Wales to reflect the different national context. They also mention the use of the NUD*IST software program for data analysis. Readers who wish to pursue further information on case-study methodology should do a search of ERIC or Wilson Web (Education) Full Text Services, and use the keywords "case study."

For readers wishing for further information on qualitative research, the following books are highly recommended: *Effective Evaluation* (1982) by E. G. Guba and Y. S. Lincoln (Jossey-Bass), *Case Study Research* (1994 or latest edition) by R. K. Yin (Sage Publications), and *Doing Qualitative Educational Research* (2001) by G. Walford (Continuum).

— 5

Quantitative methods: descriptive studies, correlation, and causal-comparative research

In the United States in the 1960s, the administration of President Lyndon Johnson launched a number of social programs collectively identified as *The War on Poverty*. The "war" included a significant first-time investment by the federal government in education aimed at reducing inequities that existed in the nation's schools. Prior to this, education in the United States was considered strictly the responsibility of the states and localities. In 1964, the US Congress allocated a portion of these funds to a study concerning the educational opportunity of children as it related to race, color, religion, and national origin. A well-respected professor from Harvard University, James Coleman, was selected to carry out this study using an extensive survey sample and sophisticated data analysis techniques. Coleman predicted that the study would show that differences in the quality of schools were the major factors retarding the academic achievement of poor and minority children (Coleman *et al.*, 1966, p. 325).

The survey sampled the academic performance and related attributes of more than 600,000 students in all 50 states. Contrary to what he had predicted, Coleman and his team concluded that school conditions had little influence on a child's academic achievement and that non-school factors such as family background, neighborhood, and peer environment were at least as influential if not more so.

Coleman's controversial report, *Equality of Educational Opportunity*, stirred the educational profession in the United States and throughout the world. Subsequent studies were conducted to confirm or refute Coleman's report. In 1972, Christopher Jencks, in a three-year study of American schools, reached essentially the same conclusions as Coleman. Jencks commented:

...children seem to be far more influenced by what happens at home than what happens in school. They also may be more influenced by what happens on the streets and by what they see on television. Everything else – the school budget, its policies, the characteristics of teachers – is either secondary or completely irrelevant. (Jencks *et al.*, 1972, p. 255)

A number of studies have since been conducted that refute Coleman and Jencks research. However, because of the large sample sizes, the tools used to collect data, and the techniques used for analysis, their benchmark studies continue to be cited decades later by many researchers and educational policy-makers.

QUANTITATIVE RESEARCH

The main topic of this chapter is quantitative research, namely descriptive studies, correlation, and causal comparative research. The story of James Coleman is an appropriate introduction to this topic because his research in the 1960s represented one of the largest quantitative studies ever conducted up until that time. Quantitative research relies on the collection of numerical data which are then subjected to analysis using statistical routines. Rather than a rich textual descriptive treatment of a subject, quantitative research provides brief presentations of distributions, tables, graphs, and formula-driven findings to describe, compare, and show relationships between and among a carefully defined set of variables. Quantitative research may be conducted on samples that range from 30 students in a single class to 300,000 students in a national sample. Material on statistical procedures appears in the appendix at the end of this primer and may be referred to during the reading of this chapter or before.

In this chapter, three of the more popular quantitative educational research methods will be explored. These three methods, descriptive studies, correlation, and causal comparative research, are referred to in some textbooks as non-experimental methods because variables are not manipulated (McMillan, 2004).

DESCRIPTIVE STUDIES

The nature of descriptive studies
The quantitative descriptive study uses numerical data to describe and interpret events, conditions, or situations that are occurring in

the present. The purpose of a descriptive study is to examine a phenomenon that is occurring at a specific place(s) and time. In many ways it is related to the case study presented in Chapter 4. However, there is a difference. The case study is a qualitative methodology that attempts to study a single subject closely and provide a rich description. Quantitative data are sometimes used to support interpretations and findings. On the other hand, a quantitative descriptive study starts with the collection of numerical data on a subject followed by a statistical analysis. Subsequently, a modest amount of qualitative data may be collected to support interpretations. The object of a quantitative descriptive study may be a single group of students in a single class, an entire school district, or a national sample. One of its major benefits is that a large sample of subjects can be examined. Designing a quantitative descriptive study for 1000 students is not very different from designing it for 50 since descriptive studies rely on surveys, questionnaires, and data collected from school databases. In most cases, the tools and analysis will be the same, while the scope of the data collection will increase (e.g., mailings, coding, and converting into electronic format).

A descriptive study can be especially effective when comparing subpopulations such as students, different schools, or different school districts. Comparative descriptive studies are popular among many educational researchers and especially government funding agencies. Critical to the design of a descriptive study that compares subpopulations is the careful identification of the variables that will be used in the analysis. Once the data have been collected, it is very difficult to collect additional data. Students move, educational policies change, or new teachers are assigned, all of which can effect data reporting.

One of the major benefits of a quantitative descriptive study is its potential for generalization. If a random sample of a larger population has been selected, a researcher can appropriately suggest that the findings be extended to the larger population.

Process and procedures in quantitative descriptive studies

The first step in planning a descriptive study is identifying a current topic that is of interest to the researcher. In general, as long as the researcher has access to data, any one of an extensive number of topics will be suitable for a descriptive study. Appropriate examples include:

- student performance and other outcomes in a class, school, or school district
- technology use in a school or school district
- teacher attitudes in a school or school district
- a comparison of teacher and staff salaries in different types of school districts: urban, suburban, rural.

In a descriptive study, hypotheses and research questions (see Figure 5.1) are stated from the onset of the research. Research questions tend to be more common than hypotheses. Examples of appropriate hypotheses are:

The implementation of the Reading Recovery Program improved student performance scores on standardized reading tests in Public School 123.
Boys make greater use of after-school technology laboratories than girls in_____.

Examples of appropriate research questions are:

What are the attitudes of teachers in the_____Charter School?

Purpose	The quantitative descriptive study uses numerical data to describe and interpret events, conditions, or situations that are occurring in the present.
Hypothesis/Research questions	Stated at the beginning of the study. Research questions tend to be used more frequently than hypotheses.
Data collection/ Sources	Quantitative data from surveys, questionnaires, and school databases.
Data analysis	Data are coded and converted into electronic form and analyzed using a computer software program such as SPSS to conduct simple descriptive analysis (e.g., frequency distributions, contingency tables, means, standard deviations).
Reporting results	Reports generally follow the standard educational research format, are brief, and to the point, Quantitative data are presented using standard formats for frequency distribution, tables, and graphs. If appropriate techniques were used to generate a random sample, the researcher can infer generalization of the findings to the larger population.

Figure 5.1. Planning for a quantitative descriptive study

How do salary schedules compare in urban, suburban, and rural school districts in California?

In quantitative research, hypotheses/research questions are stated specifically early on and remain fairly constant throughout the study. This is in contrast to qualitative research, where hypotheses/research questions are stated broadly and evolve and change as data are collected and analyzed.

An important part of the planning for a descriptive study is to determine what data may readily be available, from a school database for example, and what new data may have to be collected through surveys or questionnaires. The researcher must obtain permission from appropriate authorities to access any official school records whether they are in paper or electronic form. The researcher must also have permission from the school district to survey students, teachers, or staff for additional data.

Once a determination of data availability has been made, the researcher develops a file layout identifying all variables that will be collected, their coding schemes, and provisions for conversion into electronic form. Data are derived from characteristics about people, places, and things. These characteristics may vary and hence are called variables. Age, gender, ethnicity, teacher satisfaction, teacher salary, student attitudes, reading achievement, mathematics achievement, test scores, and grade point averages are all examples of variables that might be used in educational research. While certain variables such as age or salary relate directly to actual numeric quantities, coding schemes may need to be established for other non-numeric or categorical variables. For example:

for gender, 1 = female, 2 = male
for school type, 1 = primary, 2 = middle, 3 = secondary
for school location, 1 = urban, 2 = suburban, 3 = rural.

A researcher generally has flexibility with developing a coding scheme depending upon the type of data being collected. Most data analysts would suggest that schemes use numeric codes as much as possible. For example, for gender rather than "f" or "m" a "1" or "2" would be preferable because subsequent statistical analysis using computer software packages may run more efficiently. Researchers not familiar with developing data file layouts and coding schemes should consult with someone with expertise early on so that problems do not occur later that might jeopardize the ability to do statistical analysis. Manuals and training materials that come with statistical software packages such as SPSS provide information on how to set up a file for data and statistical analysis. The US National Center for Educational Statistics also maintains a website at: <http://nces.ed.gov/pubs2000/studenthb/> that contains a data element dictionary including coding schemes for a comprehensive student data file. Figure 5.2 shows part of a sample layout for a student data file. It is similar to the type of file layout used in SPSS.

If a survey is needed to collect all or part of the data, readers should review the material in Chapter 3. Especially important is the decision whether or not a random sample will be drawn from a larger population. The size of the sample is the researcher's

Variable ID	Type	Width	Decimals	Value code	Notes
Student ID	Numeric	9	0		
School ID	Numeric	5	0		
Gender	Numeric	1	0	1 = Female 2 = Male	
Birthdate	Numeric	6	0		YY/MM/DD
Race	Numeric	1	0	1 = Native American 2 = Asian 3 = Black 4 = Pacific Islander 5 = White	
Born outside the USA	Numeric	1	0	1 = Yes 2 = No 3 = Unknown	
Citizenship	Numeric	1	0	1 = Dual, national 2 = Nonresident alien 3 = Resident alien 4 = US citizen 5 = Other	
Country of origin	Alphabetic	15			
Family income	Numeric	7	0		
Grade-point average	Numeric	4	2		e.g., 3.25, 4.00

Figure 5.2 Excerpt of a student file layout

decision. Generally, the larger the random sample the more representative of the total population. However, the larger samples incur higher costs in both money and time in printing, mailing, coding, and converting responses. If the researcher intends to make inferences from the survey sample to a total population, then it is imperative that a truly random sample be drawn.

Data analysis requires the careful coding and conversion of all data into electronic form for processing with a statistical software package. When all data have been converted, the researcher should run a series of simple statistical procedures such as frequency distributions and contingency tables to become familiar with the data file. The researcher should do a very careful edit to be sure that key variables are accurate. For example, if a number of statistical procedures will be used to examine or control for type of school (e.g., 1 = primary, 2 = middle, 3 = secondary) then all entries for type of school should be reviewed and corrected for mistakes. SPSS and most statistical software packages have procedures for handling missing data values.

Once the data file has been edited, the researcher is ready to run statistical procedures to analyze the data. Frequency distributions, contingency tables, analyses of means and standard deviations are common in descriptive studies. Sharing initial findings with someone who is familiar with the topic or procedures being used may help in interpretation.

In presenting results and writing a report, a very brief description of the setting and subjects is common. A clear description of the methodology is expected. The bulk of the report should be devoted to a presentation and interpretation of the statistical analyses. Tables, graphs, and other numeric presentations should be carefully designed and consistent throughout the report. It should be assumed that the readers know very little about the statistical procedures being used and every effort should be made to explain them. This not only helps the reader to understand the report but also establishes the expertise of the researcher. In presenting findings and results, the researcher should also provide the rationales applied in interpreting the data. If a random sample was drawn, the researcher can make careful inferences from the findings to the larger population.

Figure 5.3 is an excerpt from the methodology section of a quantitative descriptive study that examined the experiences and perceptions of principals in the state of Virginia regarding the growing shortage of school administrators. The excerpt describes

This excerpt is taken from an article entitled "The principalship at a crossroads: a study of the conditions and concerns of principals" by Michael DiPaola and Megan Tschannen-Moran. It was published by *NASSP Bulletin* **87**: 43–65, Mar. 2003. The entire article is available on the Internet from Wilson Web (Education) Full Text Services.

Method

To obtain a view of the principalship through the eyes of current practitioners, a survey was developed to capture their concerns. This study was limited to principals in Virginia. ... An advisory board that comprised two primary researchers, the executive directors of the two principal associations in the state (Virginia Association of Secondary School Principals [VASSP] and the Virginia Association of Elementary School Principals [VAESP]), as well as elementary, middle, and high school principals was established to design the survey for this study. The advisory board prioritized and selected survey items from a pool of possible items compiled by the researchers and added additional questions of their own. The result was a seven-page survey with 176 questions that queried respondents about the conditions and challenges of their work as principals.

Participants

Questionnaires were mailed to 4,237 principals and assistant principals (APs) in the state of Virginia with a cover letter from the director of their respective professional association. The mailed directions gave participants the option of completing the survey on paper or on-line at a website designed for this purpose. Two weeks later, follow-up postcards were mailed to the recipients. ... The surveys were anonymous, thus it was not possible to contact non-respondents to see whether they differed in any systematic way from those who did respond. ... A total of 1,666 useable surveys were returned (1,406 paper surveys and 236 electronically submitted surveys). However, 83 responses were removed because they either did not indicate a position title (n = 20), or the "other" designation was selected indicating that the respondent was not currently acting in the role of principal or assistant principal (n = 63). The final useable total was 1,543 surveys for a response rate of 38%, which is a reasonable response rate for a mail survey, especially for one that is lengthy....

Data Analysis

Data analysis consisted of descriptive statistics, either of the full sample or of subsets of the sample to make comparisons between principals and assistants or between school levels (e.g., elementary, middle, and high schools). The results are reported here under five general headings: preparation for the principalship, conditions of employment, problems or issues in the field, the changing role of the principal, and supply and demand....

Figure 5.3 Sample methodology from a quantitative descriptive study

the way the survey was designed and the procedures used for following-up and editing the survey responses. Readers who wish to pursue further information on quantitative descriptive studies should do a search of ERIC or Wilson Web (Education) Full Text Services, using keywords "descriptive statistics."

CORRELATIONAL RESEARCH

The nature of correlational studies
Correlational research uses numerical data to explore the relationship between two or more variables. The exploration of the relationship between the variables provides insight into the nature of the variables themselves as well as an understanding of their relationships. Furthermore, if the relationships are substantial and consistent, they enable the researcher to make certain predictions about the variables. The purpose of correlational research therefore is to describe relationships and to predict future events based on these relationships. A correlational study may be designed to meet one or both of these purposes.

The fundamental statistical measure used in correlation is a coefficient which varies between -1.00 and +1.00. There are a number of different methods and formulae for calculating this coefficient depending upon the type of data being analyzed. One of the more commonly used is the Pearson product moment coefficient (also known as the Pearson r) which requires two sets of values that represent continuous, interval data such as standardized test scores and grade-point averages. A negative coefficient (less than 0.00) indicates an inverse correlation that is, as one variable changes (increases or decreases), the other changes in the opposite direction. A positive coefficient (greater than 0.00) indicates that as one variable changes, the other changes in the same direction. A coefficient of 0.00 indicates that there is no relationship between the variables. The design of a correlational study centers on gathering numerical data that can be analyzed to generate a coefficient(s). For example, if the researcher wants to examine the relationship between Scholastic Aptitude Test (SAT) scores and performance in college, SAT scores and grade-point averages can be collected for a representative sample of college students and subjected to a correlational analysis. If the resulting correlation coefficient is greater than 0.00, a positive relationship exists between SAT scores and college grade-point average. This means that the higher the score on the SAT, the higher the college grade-point average; the opposite is also true. If the correlation is less than 0.00, an inverse correlation exists between SAT scores and college grade-point average. This means that the higher the SAT score, the lower the college grade-point average. Besides direction (positive or inverse), the other important aspect of the correlation is the magnitude of the relationship. The closer to 1.00 or -1.00 the coefficient, the stronger the relationship. This will be discussed further in the next section of this chapter.

It is important to remember in doing correlational studies that a relationship does not necessarily indicate causality. There can be substantive correlations between two variables without one variable causing the other to happen. For example, if one were to study the relationship between student participation in extracurricular activities and student performance, one might find a high correlation but participation in extracurricular activities does not cause high performance. Perhaps other variables related to participation in extracurricular activities such as self-esteem and a positive attitude toward school might cause highly participative students to work harder and therefore to perform well.

In a correlational study designed to predict events related to two variables, one variable is identified as the predictor or independent variable while the other variable is identified as the criterion or dependent variable. The value of the predictor or independent variable is used to predict the value of the criterion or dependent variable. In the example regarding SAT score and college grade-point average, assume the relationship was positive and that as the SAT score increases, the college grade-point average increases. A simple linear model could be developed that would use the SAT score (predictor or independent variable) to predict college grade-point average (criterion or dependent variable).

Process and procedures in correlational research
The first step in planning a correlational study is to identify a topic of interest by the researcher that centers on the importance of the relationship between two or more variables. In education, many topics are amenable to a correlational study including:

- the relationship between parental involvement and student performance as measured by test scores or grade-point averages
- the relationship between student participation in extracurricular activities and student performance as measured by test scores or grade-point averages

- the relationship between student self-esteem and student performance as measured by test scores or grade-point averages
- the relationship between teacher efficacy and teacher salary
- the relationship between administrative style and school culture.

Once a topic has been selected, the researcher needs to assess the availability of quantifiable data suitable for a correlational analysis.

Either hypotheses or research questions (see Figure 5.4) can be used in a correlational study. However, null hypotheses are very common. Examples of appropriate hypotheses/research questions are:

There is no relationship between student participation in extracurricular activities and student performance as measured by test scores or grade-point averages.

There is no relationship between parental involvement and student performance as measured by test scores or grade-point averages.

What is the relationship between teacher efficacy and teacher salary?

Purpose	The correlational study uses numerical data to describe the relationship between two or more variables; and to make predictions about events associated with these variables.
Hypothesis/Research questions	Stated at the beginning of the study. The null hypothesis is frequently used.
Data collection/ Sources	Quantitative data from surveys, test scores, questionnaires, and school databases.
Data analysis	Data are coded and converted into electronic form and analyzed using a computer software program such as SPSS to conduct correlation analysis using correlation coefficients and regression.
Reporting results	Reports generally follow the standard educational research format, are brief, and to the point, Quantitative data are presented using Pearson product moment correlation coefficients, scattergrams, and regression tables. If appropriate techniques were used to generate a random sample, the researcher can infer generalization of the findings to the larger population.

Figure 5.4 Planning for a correlational study

What is the relationship between administrative style and school culture?

In a correlational study, hypotheses/research questions are stated specifically early on and remain fairly constant throughout the study. The word "relationship" is frequently used in the hypothesis or research question.

Data for a correlational study rely heavily on surveys, test scores, questionnaires, student records, and school databases. An important part of the planning for a correlational study is to determine what data are readily available (e.g., test scores from a school database) and what new data may have to be collected through surveys or questionnaires. The researcher must obtain permission from appropriate authorities to access any official school records whether they are in paper or electronic form and to survey students, teachers, and staff for additional data.

Once a determination of data availability has been made, the researcher develops a file layout which identifies all variables to be collected, determines the coding schemes, and makes provision for their conversion into electronic form. This procedure is identical to that described above for a quantitative descriptive study. While correlational studies can be conducted on many types of data including categorical, dichotomous, and ranked data, continuous interval data are the most popular format for a correlational study because they represent a large range of values within some interval scale. Examples include: the verbal portion of an SAT score can be a value between 200 and 800; the four-point grade-point average can be a value between 0.00 and 4.00; and any test or survey instrument that generates a score that has a large range of values (e.g., 1 to 100). One common research design is to collect two sets of continuous data. For example, one set of data might be the results of a survey of the television viewing habits of high-school students that reports the weekly number of hours watching television; a second set of data might be grade-point average. A Pearson product moment coefficient is then used to analyze the relationship between the two sets of data. If the Pearson r is greater than 0.00, then there is a positive relationship between the two variables which indicates that as television viewing increases so does grade-point average. On the other hand, if the Pearson r is less than 0.00, then there is an inverse relationship between the two variables which indicates that as television viewing increases, grade-point average decreases.

It is common to get some relationship between two sets of data. It is the responsibility of the researcher to determine the magnitude of the relationship. There are several procedures which can be used. Software packages such as SPSS and SAS will automatically do a test of statistical significance when doing a calculation for Pearson r. The researcher can look at the level of statistical significance (e.g., .05) and determine whether it is significant or not at the chosen level. A second method of determining the magnitude of the relationship is to use another measure called the coefficient of determination, which is simply the Pearson r squared or multiplied by itself. The coefficient of determination shows how much the relationship of the two variables is explained by the analysis. For example, in a correlation analysis a Pearson r of .50 would have a coefficient of determination of .25 (.50 × .50 = .25) This indicates that the two variables have 25 percent in common or explained by their relationship. Stated another way, if you know the value of one variable, you can predict with about 25 percent accuracy the value of the other variable. In correlational studies, the use of a coefficient of determination is also referred to as a test of practical significance. Such a test is highly recommended when establishing the magnitude of correlation.

A researcher might also decide to determine a level of magnitude testing depending upon the nature of the study. For example, a correlational study that seeks to establish the reliability of a new standardized test might require correlation coefficients higher than .80. On the other hand, a basic exploratory correlational study looking to determine a relationship between teenage smoking and school performance might accept lower correlations in the .30 to .40 range.

When relying strictly on statistical significance, the researcher is cautioned that the larger the sample, the easier it is to generate a statistically significant correlation. For example, all other things being equal, a sample of 20 subjects would need a correlation of .44 to be statistically significant at the .05 level while a sample of 100 subjects would only need a correlation of .20 to be statistically significant. In doing correlational studies, statisticians have long known that to generate statistical significance, all a researcher has to do is collect a large enough sample.

Another caveat in using the Pearson r and other forms of the correlation coefficient to show relationships or to make predictions is that they work best with linear relationships, that is, as one variable gets larger, the other gets larger (or smaller) in direct proportion. They do not work as well with curvilinear relationships in which the relationship does not follow a straight line. An example of a curvilinear relationship is age and health care. The relationship does not follow a straight line such that the older one is, the more health care one needs. Young children and older people both tend to use much more health care than teenagers or young adults. For curvilinear relationships, other statistical techniques such as multiple regression need to be used.

If a survey is needed to collect data, readers should review the material in Chapter 3 as well as the material in this chapter in the section on descriptive studies. If the researcher intends to make inferences from the survey sample to a total population, then it is imperative that a random sample be drawn.

In presenting results and writing a report, a very brief description of the setting and subjects is common. Most of the report should be devoted to the methodology, and to a presentation and interpretation of the statistical analyses. Tables, graphs, and other numeric presentations should be carefully designed and consistent throughout the report. In presenting findings and results, the researcher should also provide the rationales applied in interpreting the data. If a random sample was drawn, the researcher may make careful inferences from the findings to the larger population.

Figure 5.5 is an excerpt from the methodology section of a correlational study that investigated the relationship between elementary preservice teachers' mathematics anxiety levels and learning style preferences. The excerpt includes descriptions of the two survey instruments used. Readers who wish to pursue further information on correlation research should search ERIC or Wilson Web (Education) Full Text Services, and use the keyword "correlation."

CAUSAL COMPARATIVE RESEARCH

The nature of causal comparative research

One limitation of correlational research is that a relationship between two variables does not indicate causality. Establishing cause and effect requires careful and rigorous research methods. Causal comparative, also known as "ex post facto" (after the fact) research, is one of the more common non-experimental methods that addresses cause and effect. It attempts to try to establish cause–effect relationships between two variables where a causal or independent variable cannot be changed or manipulated. For example, certain personal characteristics such as race and ethnicity, which

This excerpt is taken from an article entitled "Mathematics anxiety and learning styles: what is the *relationship* in elementary preservice teachers?" by Tina Sloan, C. J. Daane, and Judy Giesen. It was published by *School Science and Mathematics*, **102**(2): 84–7, Fall 2002. The entire article is available on the Internet from Wilson Web (Education) Full Text Services.

The study involved 72 elementary preservice teachers (66 females and 6 males) at a mid-sized southeastern U.S. university. Sixty-one were elementary education (K-6) majors, while 11 were majoring in special education. Sixty-nine were Caucasian, while 1 each was African–American, Native American, and Asian. All had completed at least two college mathematics courses.

Two instruments were used to obtain the data: the Mathematical Anxiety Rating Scale (MARS) and the Style Analysis Survey (SAS). The MARS is a 98-item instrument consisting of brief everyday-life and academic situations pertaining to mathematics (Suinn, 1972). The instrument uses a Likert scale with a range of not at all to very much. A total score is calculated by assigning a value of 1 (low anxiety) to 5 (high anxiety) to each item and then adding the values. Richardson and Suinn (1972) reported a test-retest reliability coefficient of .97. . . .

The SAS is a 110-item instrument designed to identify how individuals prefer to learn, concentrate, and perform in both educational and work environments (Oxford, 1990). The instrument has 11 subscales and uses a Likert Scale with the following responses: 0 = never; 1 = sometimes; 2 = very often; and 3 = always. . . . The subscales are combined into five major categories: (a) Category 1 – using physical senses (visual, auditory, hands-on), (b) Category 2 – dealing with people (extroverted, introverted), (c) Category 3 – handling possibilities (intuitive, concrete-sequential), (d) Category 4 – approaching tasks (closure-oriented, open), and (e) Category 5 – dealing with ideas (global, analytic). Scores for each of the five categories are determined by summing the values of 0 to 3 assigned to each of the 10 items related to the category. If the scores in each category are within 2 points of each other, subjects are considered to be combinations of each category. For example, subjects may be categorized as global, analytic, or global/analytic depending on the closeness of their scores.

In order to determine if there was a correlation between mathematics anxiety and learning styles, a correlation was done between the MARS and the SAS. Scores obtained from the MARS and each of the SAS subscales were analyzed using Pearson product-moment correlations.

Figure 5.5 Sample methodology from a correlational study

cannot be changed, may affect an educational outcome such as student achievement. Generally the independent variable refers to events or conditions which have already occurred. Suppose a research project involved stress or burnout (effect variable) of regular education and special education teachers in a particular school setting. Since the researcher cannot manipulate the licenses and assignments of teachers (causal variable), he or she might survey or interview a sample of regular and special education teachers to determine their level of stress or burnout.

To establish a cause–effect relationship in causal comparative research, it is necessary to build a persuasive logical argument that the independent variable is affecting the dependent variable. Critical to this argument is convincing the reader that other uncontrolled extraneous variables have not had an effect on the dependent variable. To this end, the researcher must be scrupulous in drawing a sample that minimizes the effects of other extraneous variables. The researcher is free to use a number of research tools and methods including qualitative research techniques to collect data. Surveys, questionnaires, test data, school databases, and interviews are all appropriate. For data analysis, descriptive statistics, correlations, and differences of means, standard deviations, and variances can be used.

Process and procedures in causal comparative research
The first step in planning a causal comparative study is identifying an effect variable which might have a relationship with another causal variable(s) which cannot be changed or manipulated. As a result of these restrictions, far fewer causal comparative studies are conducted than other non-experimental research designs. Topics appropriate for causal comparative research include:

- the effects of socioeconomic variables such as gender, race, ethnicity on student learning styles
- the effects of class size on teacher attitudes
- the effects of teacher certification on student performance
- the effects of gender on the student use of technology in classroom activities.

In selecting a topic, the researcher must determine that the causal variable cannot be manipulated. If it can be manipulated, the researcher should consider another research design such as experimental research.

Hypotheses and research questions (see Figure 5.6) in a causal comparative study are established at the very beginning of the study. In most cases, hypotheses are used. Examples of appropriate hypotheses are:

Student socioeconomic factors have no effect on student performance as measured by standardized tests.
Class size has no effect on teacher attitudes toward students.
The credentialing (certification) of teachers has no effect on student performance.
Gender has no effect on technology laboratory use of middle-school boys and girls.

In stating a hypothesis in a causal comparative study, the word "effect" is frequently used.

Data for a causal comparative study may be collected from a number of sources including surveys, test scores, questionnaires, student records, and school databases. Qualitative techniques, especially interviews, may also be used. A critical part of the planning for a causal comparative study is to identify two or more samples of subjects that are different in some measurable and potentially educationally important way. For example, an effect

Purpose	The purpose of causal comparative research is to try to establish cause-and-effect relationships between two variables where the causal variable cannot be manipulated.
Hypothesis/Research questions	Stated at the beginning of the study. Hypotheses are generally used.
Data collection/ Sources	Quantitative data from surveys, test scores, questionnaires, and school databases. Qualitative techniques, especially interviews, can also be used to gather insights/data for building a persuasive argument linking the causal and effect variables.
Data analysis	Data are coded and converted into electronic form and analyzed using a computer software program such as SPSS. The researcher is free to use a number of analytical procedures including descriptive statistics, correlations, and differences of means and variances.
Reporting results	Reports generally are lengthy. A good description of the nature of the cause-and-effect topic being studied is required. In addition, the researcher builds a persuasive logical argument linking the causal variable(s) to the effect variable. Quantitative data and qualitative data (if used) are presented to support the argument.

Figure 5.6 Planning for a causal comparative study

variable such as student performance on a standardized test, grade-point average, or some other measure can be easily collected from school records. These data can be categorized by ranking performance scores into low, medium, and high performers. Data on a causal variable such as a student characteristic (gender, race, ethnicity, second-language learner) are also collected. Statistical comparisons can then be made on both variables to determine the extent of the cause-and-effect relationship between the two if any. In drawing samples, the researcher assures that the subjects are similar in all other extraneous characteristics that might affect outcomes such as school type or school location. As with other methodologies, the researcher must obtain permission from appropriate authorities to access any official school records whether they are in paper or electronic form.

Once a determination of data availability has been made, the researcher develops a file layout identifying all variables that will be collected, determines coding schemes, and makes provisions for conversion into electronic form. This procedure is identical to that described above for a quantitative descriptive study. The researcher is free to use various quantitative or qualitative techniques to build the case that there is a cause-and-effect relationship. Correlation coefficients and regression analysis can be used to show relationships between causal and effect variables. However, analyses of the means, standard deviations, and variances of the samples are also frequently used to add support to the correlation findings. The use of multiple statistical techniques is highly encouraged to build a persuasive argument that the cause of the effect (e.g., student performance) is due to a certain uncontrollable causal variable (e.g., student characteristic).

A causal comparative research report is usually lengthier than reports resulting from other quantitative methodologies. A description of the setting and subjects is included. Most of the report is devoted to building a persuasive argument that a cause-and-effect relationship exists in the sample. Researchers should use language that suggests the cause-and-effect relationship rather than makes an outright claim that it is so. Rationales, logic, and insights for building the argument should all be presented as clearly and as thoroughly as possible. Caution is recommended in making inferences based on the causal comparative findings to the larger population.

Figure 5.7 is an excerpt from the methodology section of a causal comparative study that investigated the effects of a block-

This excerpt is taken from an article entitled "Effects of block scheduling on academic achievement among high school students" by Charlotte D. Gruber and Anthony J. Onwuegbuzie. It was published by *The High School Journal* **84**(4): 32–42, April/May 2001. The entire article is available on the Internet from Wilson Web (Education) Full Text Services.

Research Design and Procedures

This research utilized a causal-comparative research design, also known as an ex post facto design (Huck, 2000). The two groups that were used in the investigation were the 1996–97 graduating class of the high school and the 1999–2000 graduating class of the high school. The 1996–97 graduating class received instruction via a traditional six-period schedule for four years of high school. On the other hand, the 1999–2000 class received instruction via a 4×4 block schedule for three years. Cumulative grade-point averages for the two groups were compared to determine if a difference in level of achievement existed between the groups. Also, Georgia High School Graduation Tests (GHSGT) scores for the 1996–97 graduating class of the high school were compared to the high school graduating class of 1999–2000 to determine if there was a statistically significant difference in achievement levels of the two cohorts. Scores for each of the five areas of the GHSGT were analyzed and compared for both of the groups. Data were included in this research for every student in the two graduating classes.

Comparing the block-schedule and the traditional-schedule students was justified because the two groups of students appeared to be similar with respect to a number of variables. In particular, qualitative analyses revealed no notable changes in the curricula in the years for which the achievement data were collected. Second, only 3% of the students who took the GHSGT in the 1999–2000 graduating class moved into the school district in their junior year, which is the year that the students take the battery of tests for the first time. Third, teacher turnover in each of the three years of block scheduling remained constant at approximately 16%. Finally, during the period for which the test score data were collected, the racial composition of students (e.g., 1997–1998 school year: 22.9% Black, 75.8% White, 0.9% Hispanic, 0.1% Asian, 0.3% Multiracial) remained stable, as did the gender composition (e.g., 1997–1998 school year: 51.8% male, 48.2% female).

Data Analysis

An independent samples t test was utilized to test the research hypothesis that students who receive instruction via a 4×4 block schedule have different levels of academic achievement, as measured by GPA, than do high school students who receive instruction via a traditional schedule.

Figure 5.7 Sample methodology from a causal comparative study

scheduling program on academic achievement. The procedures indicate that the causal variable (students registered in block or traditional schedule) had already occurred and could not be manipulated. The authors emphasize that the two populations appeared to be similar with respect to a number of variables including curriculum, teacher turnover, gender, and race. Readers who might wish to pursue further information on correlation research may search ERIC or Wilson Web (Education) Full Text Services, and use the keyword "causal comparative" or "ex post facto."

For readers wishing for further information on quantitative research, the following are highly recommended: *Research Methods in Education: An Introduction* (2000 or latest edition) by W. Wiersma (Allyn and Bacon) and *Quantitative Methods in Educational Research* (2001) by S. Gorard (Continuum).

Experimental studies

Robert Slavin, a well-known educator, started his career as a social studies teacher and worked with special education children in the early 1970s. In 1975, he decided to pursue an educational research career shortly after receiving his Ph.D. from Johns Hopkins University. Among his early research interests was cooperative learning.

In 1979, he published "Effects of biracial learning teams on cross-racial friendships" in the *Journal of Educational Psychology*. This experimental study took place in two Baltimore inner city junior high schools. Five teachers and 420 seventh and eighth-grade students comprised 12 English classes studying a ten-week unit on grammar, punctuation, and English usage. A cooperative learning approach called Student Teams Achievement Divisions (STAD) was used in six classes and six classes served as a control group. Teachers and students in either group were not aware that they were part of an experiment involving race relations. All participants were told that the experiment involved two different instructional methods; but were not made aware that they were part of experimental or control groups. Pre and posttests were administered using a simple sociometric measure consisting of one question: "Who are your friends in this class?" Provision was made for 22 names. Statistical procedures included two multiple regression analyses and factorial analysis.

The study was well designed and can serve as a model for conducting experimental research. The same content was taught in both groups. Teachers and students were not aware of whether they were experimental or control or of the nature of the experiment. The data-collection instrument was simple to administer. The statistical procedures were rigorous. Furthermore, the study added to our knowledge of cooperative learning. Despite its exemplary aspects, Dr. Slavin lamented that the follow-up data collection was problematic. At the end of the ten-week experiment, posttests were collected from 294 participants or approximately 70 percent of the original sample. In follow-up testing, nine months later, only 36 (8.5 percent) of the original 420 participants were available. Dr. Slavin attributed the attrition to high absenteeism, high transience, and difficulty in separating students who had been in the earlier study from those who had not. He observed that these were common problems when working in schools with highly mobile student populations. This vignette points to an important lesson for any educational researcher: even the best-designed research projects may encounter unforeseen problems.

Dr. Slavin went on to a stellar career in education. He has published more than 200 articles and 15 books including two on educational research. He received the American Educational Research Association's (AERA) Raymond B. Cattell Early Career Award for Programmatic Research in 1986, the Palmer O. Johnson Award for the best article in an AERA journal in 1988, the Charles A. Dana Award for pioneering achievement in 1994, the James Bryant Conant Award from the Education Commission of the States in 1998, and the Outstanding Educator Award from the Horace Mann League in 1999. At the time of this writing, he is Co-Director of the Center for Research on the Education of Students Placed at Risk at Johns Hopkins University and Chairman of the Success for All Foundation.

EXPERIMENTAL RESEARCH

Experimental research has been referred to as the "gold standard of research design" because it seeks to study and establish cause and effect (Gorard, 2001, p. 193). None of the other methodologies with the exception of causal comparative research can make this claim. Experimental research is, in many ways, the most formal of educational research designs although there are variations of this method that allow researchers to use experimental techniques without employing the full rigor of a true experiment. *Quasi-experimental* research has evolved and has become popular especially when conducted in natural settings (e.g., schools, classrooms). In the following paragraphs, the true experimental design will be presented followed by several less rigorous variations. Issues of validity and experimental controls will also be discussed.

The nature of experimental research

The purpose of experimental research is to study cause (independent variable) and effect (dependent variable) relationships between two or more variables where the causal variable can be manipulated. In a classic example of a true experiment in education, two randomly selected groups of students are similar in key characteristics: one group (experimental) is taught for a period of time using a new technique or treatment; and a second group (control or placebo) is taught using a traditional technique. At the conclusion of the experiment, the two groups are tested to determine if there is a difference in their achievement. The teaching technique represents the causal or independent variable and student achievement is the effect or dependent variable. The causal variable in this example has been manipulated by assigning students to two groups in which different teaching methods are used. In analyzing the test results, if student achievement was greater in the experimental group, then the researcher can claim that the new teaching technique (treatment) was the cause.

This type of experiment represents a basic experimental research model which has been conducted many times. Although the technique appears to be relatively simple, most researchers will encounter a number of issues that might make it difficult for them to conduct the experiment. For instance, one question might be: "Do we really want to experiment with the achievement of children?" Suppose the experiment outlined above was conducted for a semester on two fourth-grade mathematics classes and suppose rather than improving achievement, the experiment showed that achievement was significantly lower for the experimental group. Who is responsible for the significantly lower achievement of these children and how do the researchers remediate the situation? This situation represents a major concern in the way experimental research is conducted as opposed to other methods where variables are not manipulated. Cook (2002) in an article entitled "Randomized experiments in educational policy research: a critical examination of the reasons the educational evaluation community has offered for not doing them" reviewed the literature and identified five broad arguments for not doing true experimental studies as follows:

1. Philosophical arguments designed to show that experiments: (a) cannot provide unbiased tests of causal hypotheses, and (b) are predicated on a descriptive theory of

causation that is less useful than explanatory theories of cause.

2. Practical arguments asserting that experiments: (a) can rarely be mounted in schools, and (b) when mounted, are often imperfectly realized because of compromises to the planned treatment contrasts and the quality of individual treatment implementation.

3. Arguments about undesirable trade-offs because experiments: (a) sacrifice external for internal validity; and (b) value causal conclusions so highly that a conservative bias results which overlooks useful findings indicated by more liberal criteria.

4. Arguments that schools will not use experimental results because: (a) experiments meet the interests of federal and state policy-makers who are not major actors in educational policy; and (b) the experiment's logic recreates a rational decision-making model that does not describe how schools actually make decisions.

5. Arguments that experiments are not necessary because better alternatives exist. These alternatives include: (a) the intensive qualitative case studies preferred by self-styled educational evaluators; (b) the quasi-experimental studies preferred by substantive researchers who value design control over statistical control; and (c) the causal modeling studies preferred by substantive researchers who do longitudinal work in education. (Cook, 2002, p. 177)

As a result of these concerns, researchers have developed a variety of techniques that preserve elements of the experimental approach while allowing for less rigorous methodologies.

Variations in the experimental design
Experimental research has spawned a number of research designs (see Figure 6.1). It is important for the researcher to be aware of these designs and select the one that will work best for the topic at hand. The major differences in these designs involve one or more of the following:

- the use of random sampling
- the use of pretesting
- the number of groups.

Although desirable, random sampling is not always possible, especially in the natural setting. Students are assigned to classes or to particular teachers for a number of sound educational reasons. Conducting a random sample experiment might be disruptive or possibly harmful so that many school administrators would be reluctant to grant permission to do so. As a result, a number of designs employing experimental methods were developed that do not depend upon random sampling. These approaches are frequently referred to as *quasi-experimental*. They are less rigorous than true experimental designs but may be more practical to conduct in the field.

Experimental design	Sample	No. of groups	Pretest	Intervention	Posttest
Two-group random pre-posttest (Classic Design)	Random	Two	Yes	Treatment in experimental group – placebo in control group	Yes
Two-group random posttest only	Random	Two	No	Treatment in experimental group – placebo in control group	Yes
Two-group nonrandom* pre-posttest	Not random	Two	Yes	Treatment in experimental group – placebo in control group	Yes
Two-group nonrandom posttest only	Not random	Two	No	Treatment in experimental group – placebo in control group	Yes
One-group random pre-posttest	Random	One	Yes	Treatment in experimental group	Yes
One-group random posttest only	Random	One	No	Treatment in experimental group	Yes
One-group nonrandom pre-posttest	Not random	One	Yes	Treatment in experimental group	Yes
One-group nonrandom posttest only	Not random	One	No	Treatment in experimental group	Yes

*Note: Nonrandom designs are referred to as nonequivalent groupings.

Figure 6.1 Variations of the experimental research design

The use of pretesting is also highly recommended in experimental research but, like random sampling, is not always possible. Some experts (McMillan, 2004; Gay, 1992; Slavin, 1992) also caution that pretesting may warn participants that they are involved in an experiment thereby possibly causing them to behave differently. The researcher must decide whether pretesting is important for the study. If it is important, procedures need to be put in place to assure that the pretesting does not tip the participants off to the nature of the experiment.

A two-group experiment is a more rigorous design than a one-group experiment. Unfortunately, circumstances in the natural setting do not always allow for a two-group design. If a one-group design is used, the researcher must exercise caution in concluding a cause-and-effect relationship. One-group designs can also be useful as a pre-experimental test to build knowledge about a technique that might subsequently be used in a two-group experimental design.

There are several other experimental research variations that are not included in Figure 6.1. For example, experimental research can be conducted using a *time series* design that requires conducting tests or measurements several times during the period of the experiment. Rather than simply pre and posttesting, testing is conducted at set intervals and progress is measured over time. Situations where testing might be used more frequently, when the experiment is being conducted for an extended period of time, or where the treatments are administered with certain achievement milestones anticipated, are conducive to such a design.

Factorial designs in experimental research are used when there is more than one independent variable. A factorial design is most appropriate when the researcher is interested in studying results across several factors or characteristics such as age, gender, race, ethnicity in addition to the treatment. This would be important if the researcher suspects that the treatment may affect subjects differently. For example, many studies that look at the effects of technology in education are frequently concerned that girls and boys respond differently. In designing an experiment involving the use of technology, it might be beneficial to study the effect of gender as well as the treatment.

Figure 6.1 describes one or two-group experimental designs. However, it is also possible, and in some cases desirable, to have a *multi-group* experiment. For example, a study to look at the effect of class size on student achievement might be designed with three groups as follows:

Experimental Group 1: class sizes 15–20 students
Experimental Group 2: class sizes 21–25 students
Experimental Group 3: class sizes 26–30 students

Statistical procedures would then be used to determine if there were differences in student achievement among the three groups.

All of the experimental designs mentioned thus far assume that there are one or more groups of students being studied. In some experiments, it might be more appropriate to study single subjects rather than groups. *Single-subject* experimental designs are common and especially useful in the study of behavior patterns or time on task. A single-subject study can be integrated with other research methods including time-series experiments and individual case study analysis (see Chapter 4). Single-subject research is important for research in areas of special education where teachers frequently work with individual students.

Before concluding this section, a brief mention should be made of standard experimental research notation. This notation uses letters and symbols to represent different experimental research procedures. In conducting reviews of the literature, a researcher may come across this notation and should be familiar with it. Experimental research designs can be represented by the following:

R = random assignment
X_n = treatment (subscripts indicate different treatments)
O = observations (including pre and posttests)
A,B,C,D = group designations

For example, a single-group design using a random sample with one treatment and pre and posttest would be represented as:

Group A   R   O X_1 O

A two-group design using a random sample with posttest only would be:

Group A   R X_1 O
Group B   R X_2 O

Figure 6.2 provides a table of various experimental research designs with their respective notations.

Experimental design	Standard research notation
Two-group random pre-posttest (classic design)	Group A R O X_1 O Group B R O X_2 O
Two-group random posttest only	Group A R X_1 O Group B R X_2 O
Two-group nonrandom* pre-posttest	Group A O X_1 O Group B O X_2 O
Two-group nonrandom posttest only	Group A X_1 O Group B X_2 O
One-group random pre-posttest	Group A R O X_1 O
One-group random posttest only	Group A R X_1 O
One-group nonrandom pre-posttest	Group A O X_1 O
One-group nonrandom posttest only	Group A X_1 O

*Note: Nonrandom designs are referred to as nonequivalent groupings.

Figure 6.2 Standard experimental research design notation

Process and procedures in experimental research
In planning an experimental study, the researcher selects a topic which can be studied as a cause-and-effect relationship. Topics appropriate for experimental research include:

- the effect of a new teaching technique on student achievement
- the effect of staff development activities on teacher morale
- the effect of cooperative learning techniques on student social maturation
- the effect of the integration of technology in classroom activities on student achievement.

In selecting a topic, the researcher makes a critical determination that the causal variable can be manipulated. If it cannot be manipulated, the researcher should consider whether the research can be conducted.

Hypotheses and research questions (see Figure 6.3) in an experimental study are established at the very beginning of the study. Hypotheses are generally used. Examples of appropriate hypotheses are:

There is no difference in the achievement of students when taught using a whole-language reading approach versus a phonics approach.
Staff development activities will have no effect on teacher morale.
Cooperative learning has a positive effect on social maturation.
Integrating technology into classroom activities has no effect on student achievement.

Purpose	The purpose of experimental research is to study cause-and-effect relationships between two variables where the causal variable can be manipulated.
Hypothesis/Research questions	Stated at the beginning of the study. Hypotheses are generally used.
Data collection/Sources	Quantitative data from test scores, attitudinal instruments, and other measurements. Researcher controls for threats to internal validity.
Data analysis	Data are coded and converted into electronic form and analyzed using a computer software program such as SPSS. The researcher is free to use a number of analytical procedures. Among the more popular are analyses of the differences in two or more groups using t tests and analysis of variance (ANOVA).
Reporting results	Reports generally follow the standard educational research format, are brief, and to the point. Clear, precise description of the methodology and procedural controls (e.g., random sampling, pre and posttesting) are expected. Quantitative data are presented using t-test and ANOVA results. The researcher can infer generalization of the findings to the larger population if threats to external validity were controlled during the period of the experiment.

Figure 6.3 Planning for an experimental study

In stating a hypothesis in experimental studies, the words "effect" and "difference" are frequently used.

Quantitative data gathered from tests, attitudinal instruments, or other measurements generally may be collected before (pretest) and after (posttest) the experiment is concluded. However, as mentioned earlier, not all experimental research designs use pretesting.

In developing data collection and other procedures for the experiment, the researcher should be aware of any threats to internal and external validity. Internal validity refers to the extent to which findings can be interpreted accurately. External validity refers to the extent to which results can be generalized to larger populations. Both forms of validity are important to several educational research methodologies but are especially critical in experimental research. Campbell and Stanley (1963) are recognized by experts (McMillan, 2004; Gay, 1992; Wiersma, 2000) in the field of experimental research as amongst the first to identify and categorize threats to internal and external validity. Figure 6.4 provides a brief summary of their work in this area. Researchers should attempt to minimize, if not eliminate, the effects of these threats on the experiment. For example, subjects should be randomly assigned whenever possible (Interaction effects of selection bias). If they are not, then the researcher must be careful of making generalizations of the findings to larger populations. Subjects should not be informed that they are part of an experiment (Reactive effects of subjects – Hawthorne effect) because they may behave differently if they know they are being observed. The Hawthorne effect is named after a series of studies conducted in the 1930s at a Western Electric plant in Hawthorne, Illinois. The studies involved the effect on worker productivity of changes in work conditions such as more illumination, less illumination, longer days, or shorter days. The findings were that regardless of the changes in work conditions, productivity increased at least temporarily. The researchers concluded that once the participants knew that they were part of a study, they became more productive regardless of the treatment. A variation of the Hawthorne effect is the *halo* effect which occurs when participants know that they are part of the experimental group and their belief that they are part of a special group pushes them to improve performance. Another variation (the opposite of the halo effect) is the John Henry effect in which participants know that they are part of the control group and make an extra effort to improve performance. The John Henry effect takes its name from the legendary railroad steel driver who exhausted himself to death

Threats to internal validity

History – environmental events that occur during the period of the experimental research which might effect the dependent variable. Example: the effect on the subjects of a national or local tragedy such as the attack on the Twin Towers on 9/11/01, or the death of a colleague or friend.

Maturation – refers to physical or mental changes that occur within the subjects over a period of time. Example: in experimental studies that last for a long time, subjects become older or better coordinated as they mature.

Testing – if pre and posttests are used, sensitization to the posttest as a result of having completed the pretest. Example: participants may learn something about a test while taking the pretest which may help their performance in a posttest.

Instrumentation – the reliability of test instruments. If different forms of the same tests are used for the pretest and the posttest and there is a suspicion that one of the tests was more difficult than the other. This happens at times with standardized tests developed by state education departments.

Statistical regression – refers to groups which are selected on the basis of their extreme (high or low) scores that tend to regress toward the mean on repeated testing. Example: subjects who score very high on a pretest tend to score lower on posttest; and subjects who score very low on a pretest tend to score higher on a posttest.

Differential selection of subjects – refers to subjects not being randomly assigned to treatment and/or control groups. Example: subject group(s) are selected because they are already formed (e.g., two fourth-grade classes in a primary school).

Mortality – refers to the loss of subjects and their data. Example: a substantive number of subjects transfer to another school or move to another environment.

Selection-maturation interaction – refers to subjects in experimental or control groups who are maturing at different rates that may effect the dependent variable. Example: in an experimental study in which subjects are of different ages such as middle school students (ages 12 through 14) who might behave differently as they grow older.

Threats to external validity

Pretest treatment interaction – subjects react differently to a treatment because they have learned something as a result of taking a pretest. Example: subjects take a pretest and learn something about the nature of the experiment and attempt to learn more about its content.

Interaction effects of selection bias – experimental groups are not randomly selected and as a result, findings cannot be generalized to larger populations. Example: an experimental group has a large percentage of low or high achievers and, as a result, findings cannot be generalized to more heterogeneous populations.

Multiple treatment interference – occurs when the same subjects participate in more than one treatment or experiment and there are unforeseen carry-over effects. Example: subjects are selected to participate in multiple studies or in similar studies in close proximity to one another. Subjects (students) participate in an experiment to learn mathematics using Method A in third grade. Some of these students are selected to participate in another experiment to learn mathematics using Method B in fourth grade. Will carry-over effects of learning Method A effect their behavior as they learn Method B?

Reactive effects of subjects – occurs when subjects know that they are participating in an experiment. Also referred to as the Hawthorne effect. Example: subjects in an experiment attempt to do better because they know they are being observed or studied.

Figure 6.4 Threats to internal and external validity in experimental research

in outperforming a new steam steel-driving machine. Key participants in an experiment, other than the subjects, should not necessarily know that they are participants because they may also behave differently. For example, teachers who are teaching as part of an experiment might teach differently if they know that they are being observed or that their students will have some special testing.

In order to analyze the data collected, the researcher needs to develop a file layout identifying all variables and coding schemes, and make provisions for their conversion into electronic form. The researcher is free to use various quantitative techniques to analyze the data. Statistical procedures such as t test and analysis of variance (ANOVA) are commonly used to determine differences in pre and posttest measures. It is highly recommended that multiple analyses of results be conducted. For example, tests of statistical significance can be followed up by tests of practical significance using effect size techniques.

In presenting results and writing a report, a very brief description of the setting and subjects is common. Most of the report is devoted to the methodology, especially the controls used, as well as to the presentation and interpretation of the statistical analyses. Tables, graphs, and other numeric presentations should be carefully designed and consistent throughout the report. In presenting findings and results, the researcher should discuss any internal validity issues germane to interpreting the data and determining the cause-and-effect relationship between variables. The researcher can generalize the findings to the larger population if threats to external validity were controled during the period of the experiment.

Figure 6.5 is an excerpt from the methodology section of an experimental study that investigated the effects of a computer software program on mathematics achievement and attitudes toward mathematics of secondary-school students. The procedures indicate that random assignment, pretesting, and controls for threats to validity were used. Campbell and Stanley are referenced regarding the random sampling. Readers who wish to pursue further information on experimental research may search ERIC or Wilson Web (Education) Full Text Services, and use the keywords "experimental study" or "quasi experimental research."

For readers wishing for further information on experimental research, the following are highly recommended: *Experimental and Quasi Experimental Designs for Research on Teaching* (1963) by D. T. Campbell and J. C. Stanley in N. L. Gage (ed.), *Handbook of Research*

This excerpt is taken from an article entitled "The effects of computer-augmented geometry instruction on student performance and attitudes" by Charles Funkhouser. It was published by the Journal of Research on Technology in *Education*, **35**(2): 163–75, Winter 2002/2003. The entire article is available on the Internet from Wilson Web (Education) Full Text Services.

METHOD

Subjects

The 49 participants in the study were enrolled in geometry courses at a large public high school in the western United States. The subjects were in either grade 10 or 11. The distribution of participants according to grade level and gender is given in Table 1.

The study was conducted over the course of two 18-week semesters. A control group consisting of 27 students was given a standardized test of geometry after instruction in plane geometry using a noncomputer-based approach. They were also given an attitude assessment both before and after the course. The treatment group consisting of 22 students was given a standardized test of geometry performance after instruction in plane geometry augmented by activities related to The Geometric Supposer (1993). Sample geometry performance test questions are given in Figure 1. Students were also given an attitude assessment both before and after the course. The items in the mathematics attitude assessment are given in Figure 2.

Both groups included a wide range of abilities. The only prerequisite at the high school for enrollment in geometry was a passing grade of at least a D in Algebra I. The comparable mathematical ability and attitudes toward mathematics of the two groups were demonstrated in two ways: (a) an analysis of student mean final grades for Algebra I and (b) a statistical analysis of the initial assessment of student attitudes. The mean final grades for the control and treatment groups were 3.17 and 3.27 (out of 4.00), respectively. A t-test of these mean scores showed that the differences were not statistically significant at the 0.05 level of significance. As shown in Table 2, results of the initial assessment of student attitudes toward mathematics suggested comparable attitudes for the two groups, except for one item. Students in the treatment group were more likely to agree with the statement "I look forward to coming to school." A t-test of differences showed a significant difference at the 0.05 level of significance.

Students were assigned to either group by computer scheduling. Though this is not strictly random assignment, Campbell and Stanley (1968) stated that this method, when used in a large school setting, comes close to random assignment.

The results of the analyses of the mean final Algebra I grades and the initial administration of the attitude assessment and the "functional" random assignment to groups diminish the likelihood that selection based on mathematical ability or disposition toward mathematics was a threat to the internal validity of this study.

Figure 6.5 Sample methodology from an experimental study

on Teaching (Rand McNally); *Educational Research: Competencies for Analysis and Application* (latest edition) by L. R. Gay (Pearson/ Merrill Education); "A reader's guide to scientifically based research" by Robert Slavin in *Educational Leadership* (February, 2003); and *Quantitative Methods in Educational Research* (2001) by S. Gorard (Continuum).

7

Action and evaluation research

In the mid-1980s, the Tennessee state legislature authorized a $12-million four-year study of class size entitled Project STAR (Student/Teacher Achievement Ratio). This longitudinal study was one of the first of its kind to analyze student achievement and development in three class types: small classes (13–17 students) with one teacher, regular classes (22–25 students) with one teacher, and regular classes (22–25) with one teacher and one full-time teacher aide. The project followed students through grade 3, starting from kindergarten (K) in 1985–6 and ending with third grade in 1988–9. It included 17 inner-city, 16 suburban, 8 urban, and 38 rural schools with a view toward assessing the effects of class size and type in different school locations. Multiple instruments were used to measure student achievement including: the Stanford Achievement Test (K–3), STAR's (grades 1–2) Basic Skills Criterion Tests, Tennessee's (grade 3) Basic Skills Criterion Tests. Student development was measured as well using the Self-Concept and Motivation Inventory.

The Executive Summary of the Project STAR report summarized the major results as follows:

1. The small classes made the highest scores on the Stanford Achievement Test (SAT) and Basic Skills First (BSF) Test in all four years (K–3) and in all locations (rural, suburban, urban, inner-city)
2. The greatest gains on the SAT were made in inner-city small classes.
3. The highest scores on the SAT and BSF were made in rural small classes.
4. The only consistent positive Regular/Aide class effect occurred in First Grade.

5. Inner-city (predominately minority) students in small classes always outscored inner-city students in regular and regular/aide classes. This suggests that small classes are very beneficial to minority students.
6. In every grade, every location, and every class type non-free lunch students outperformed free lunch students.
7. Non-free lunch minorities in suburban small classes performed as well as non-free lunch whites. (Word *et al.*, 1990)

The study was hailed as a landmark by educational policy-makers and researchers alike. Frederick Mosteller (1999), professor emeritus of mathematical statistics at Harvard University, referred to Project STAR as "one of the great experiments in education in U.S. history." More importantly, Project STAR was cited in discussions about class size in government policy-making bodies throughout the United States. Many states as well as the federal government launched class-size reduction initiatives based in part on its findings. Project STAR still stands as one of the major examples of how well-funded quality research can influence educational policy.

ACTION AND EVALUATION RESEARCH

Project STAR can be classified as a prime example of educational evaluation since action and evaluation research are designed to affect what happens in the "real world" of schools and classrooms.

Action and evaluation research focus on the development, implementation, and testing of a program, product, or procedure. They frequently are part of a grant or special program in which funds have been received by a school to test a new instructional or administrative approach. They almost always occur in school settings and are frequently conducted by or with the assistance of teachers, administrators, and other practitioners. While related, action and evaluation research are slightly different:

- Action research studies problems at the local level. It usually focuses on the development, implementation, and testing of a new product, program, plan, or procedure in a school building.
- Evaluation research is done to determine the merits of a product, process, or approach used in education.

The characteristics of action and evaluation research projects can vary significantly and frequently they will not follow the standard report format (purpose, hypothesis, methodology, findings) that we usually see with other research studies. There is a certain amount of overlap between the two methodologies as well, and many studies have been conducted which mix and match the two. These and other aspects of action and evaluation research will be examined in this chapter.

ACTION RESEARCH

The nature of action research
Debate exists as to whether action research is in fact a separate research methodology. Some popular textbooks on educational research do not equate it to experimental, causal comparative, or descriptive methods (Gay, 1992; Slavin, 1992; McMillan 2004). It can be argued that it is simply educational research applied to real-life problems in schools; that it is conducted either by or in collaboration with practitioners (teachers, counselors, school leaders); and that it depends upon other research methodologies. The origins of action research are not clear but can be traced to a number of individuals and movements. Kurt Lewin, a German social psychologist, who came to the United States in the early 1930s, is frequently associated with combining basic (theoretical) research and applied research in the social sciences, and emphasizing the importance of collaborating with actual practitioners in the field if research is to assist in social improvements and reforms.

In education, action research is associated with school-based studies that seek to improve performance and to solve problems. The purpose of action research is to improve school functions including teaching, learning, counseling, and administration. Any research methodology (qualitative or quantitative) can be adopted, statistical procedures may be used or not, or methodologies may be mixed and matched to meet its goals. In this respect, action research frequently is considered the least rigorous of the educational research methodologies. In addition, because it is so integrated into an individual school setting, it can rarely be generalized to larger populations.

Action research is frequently team-oriented. While individual teachers can conduct an action research project in their classes, it is very common to see a team of teachers and/or administrators working on a project. If sophisticated methodologies are to be used or if specific expertise is needed, an outside consultant can be added to the research team.

Process and procedures in action research

While action research allows the researcher a good deal of flexibility in the study design, its structure and process resembles the scientific method discussed in Chapter 2. Sagor (2000) describes a seven-step "disciplined process of inquiry" for conducting action research as follows:

1. Select a topic, focus, or problem
2. Clarify theories, values, and beliefs related to the topic
3. Identify research questions
4. Collect data
5. Analyze data
6. Report results
7. Take an informed action.

The last step in the process differentiates action research from most other methodologies; there is an expectation that some action will occur as a result of the research.

Almost any topic or issue is appropriate for action research. While much of action research examines instruction, other areas such as budgeting, personnel decisions, and counseling are just as appropriate. Pilot projects and grant-funded activities are especially popular for action research. These might include:

- using a new instructional technique or strategy
- examining a staff development initiative
- developing new test instruments to assess student emotional or psychological needs
- developing a new class-scheduling approach (e.g., block programming)
- using technology to streamline an administrative process.

Critical to selecting a topic for action research is its potential for leading to some improvement in the school setting.

Research questions (see Figure 7.1) are almost always used rather than hypotheses. They can be stated as generally or as specifically as the researcher thinks appropriate. Examples of research questions that can be used in action research are:

How does a new mathematics program based on the use of manipulatives effect student achievement in Intermediate School 123?
What have been the effects of a new after-school teacher

development program on improving curriculum decisions at
Public School 456?

What have been the savings in administrative costs in using a
new automated purchasing system in Public School 789?

What have been the effects of block programming on student
achievement at Westbury High School?

In each of the above examples, the research is localized to a particular school.

Purpose	The purpose of action research is to seek to improve performance and to solve problems in the local school setting.
Hypothesis/Research questions	Research questions are almost always used instead of hypotheses. They are stated broadly and usually early on as part of the research planning process.
Data collection/Sources	Qualitative and quantitative data can be collected. School records, surveys, and questionnaires are very popular.
Data analysis	Qualitative data can be analyzed using any tools appropriate to the data collection method. Likewise any quantitative data can be analyzed using a computer software program such as SPSS, usually to conduct simple descriptive analysis (e.g., frequency distributions, means, standard deviations).
Reporting results	Relatively brief reports are prepared that are shared within a school community. The format of these reports is frequently informal and does not follow a rigid research report format. Sometimes action researchers wish to share their work with a larger professional community and will publish reports of their findings in journals. In these cases, the reports should be more formally organized. Since action research concentrates on an activity in a specific school, the researcher should not try to infer that the findings can be generalized to larger populations.

Figure 7.1 Planning for action research

Data collection can utilize either qualitative or quantitative
designs or both. Case study methods are particularly popular for
action research. Quantitative data gathered from student records,
surveys, and questionnaires are also common. The rigid control

procedures generally in place in other methodologies may be relaxed in action research as researchers take advantage of approaches that integrate easily into their local school environments. Nevertheless, Sagor (2000) recommends establishing a certain amount of discipline in gathering data for an action research project. He specifically suggests using triangulation or gathering data from multiple sources to reduce bias. In the Project STAR evaluation study, for example, three different instruments were used to gather data on student outcomes. Triangulation is discussed in more detail in Chapter 4.

Data-analysis procedures should be appropriate to the data-gathering techniques used. Qualitative data analysis procedures (discussed in Chapter 4) are common. The researcher should conduct a careful review of field notes gathered from observations or interviews, audio or videotape, and any other documentation that might have been collected and summarize them as needed. If quantitative data are collected, they should be converted to electronic form and analyzed using a statistical software package. Descriptive statistics especially frequency distributions, contingency tables, means, and standard deviations are common. Analyses should be shared with other educators in the school setting who might provide insight. School administrators such as principals and superintendents especially may be in positions to provide a broader perspective on the data.

Action-research report presentations do not necessarily follow a strict research report format. For internal (school) distribution, reports can be brief and to the point. Formal reports that might be published or circulated outside the school will be lengthier. For example, a more detailed description of the setting and subjects is generally needed for external readers to understand and appreciate the nature of the action-research project. Consistency of quantitative presentations (e.g., tables, graphs, statistical findings) is considered good report design regardless of the audience.

Figures 7.2 and 7.3 are excerpts from two action-research projects. The excerpts show two different methodologies (qualitative and quantitative) for conducting action-research projects. The excerpt in Figure 7.2 is from a project which examines the development of one ESL (English as a Second Language) student. This action-research project describes a qualitative approach using a combination of interviews, observation, and literature reviews. Figure 7.3 is an excerpt from a program which was a grant-funded activity designed to integrate technology into a social studies curriculum.

Here the author relies on a quantitative approach using quasi-experimental research techniques.

Readers who wish to pursue further information on action-research methodology should do a search of ERIC or Wilson Web (Education) Full Text Services and use keywords "action research."

This excerpt is taken from an article entitled "Action research in the classroom: assisting a linguistically different learner with special needs" by Sharon Faith Schoen and Alexis Ann Schoen. It was published in *Teaching Exceptional Children*, **35**(3): 16–21, Jan./Feb. 2003. The entire article is available on the Internet from Wilson Web (Education) Full Text Services.

At the onset of the action research, Andy was administered the Botel and Dolch Sight Word Tests. On the Botel test, Andy received 95% accuracy at the pre-primer level and 65% at the primer level. The level of accuracy decreased to 50% at the first-grade level. On the Dolch test, Andy scored 82% at the primer level and 71% at the first-grade level, respectively.

Informal assessments revealed functioning in phonetic, comprehension, and writing skills. These assessments included writing samples, classroom work-sheets, and teacher-made tests. Andy's writing samples showed that he is able to understand the events or facts that are being taught, but he cannot use written language correctly to express what he is thinking. Many of his errors occur in sentence structure and spelling. For example, Andy will write, "Kirsten out of her gym bag she pok the hos and Gilbert make a los nost." (Kirsten out of her gym bag she poked the holes and Gilbert make a loud noise.) The main idea is evident in the sentence, but the structure does not make sense. Andy has success with the class sight-word list, but has more difficulty with other words. Andy will use some of his phonics skills when he is reading, but will not use them as often in his writing.

... The research question became obvious. How could Andy's language skills be more expediently developed within the context of the classroom?

STEP 2: COLLECTING DATA
A myriad of resources served to inform decision making and action planning. First, we conducted interviews with the ESL teacher, Andy's parents, and Andy himself about Andy's current functioning and learning preferences. We then investigated cultural differences, personality differences, and learning differences of students in the classroom. Last, we conducted a literature review for effective ESL strategies...

Figure 7.2 Sample description of the data-collection methods used in an action-research project

EVALUATION RESEARCH

The nature of evaluation research

Evaluation research is concerned with determining the merits of a product, process, or approach used in education. It is similar to

This excerpt is taken from an article entitled "Using technology in a middle school social studies classroom" by A. Keith Dils. It was published in the *International Journal of Social Education*, **15**(1): 102–12, Spring/Summer 2000. The entire article is available on the Internet from Wilson Web (Education) Full Text Services.

ACTION RESEARCH EVALUATING FUNDED PROJECT
In order to assess the effectiveness of this constructivist approach, the Democratic Values Inventory was developed. The inventory consists of a ten-question Likert scale survey designed to test the democratic values of eighth grade students. After the test was reviewed by colleagues for clarity and accuracy, it was then given to all 135 eighth grade students. In order to measure any change in student attitudes about democratic participation, the inventory was administered before the elections unit as a pretest and then again as a posttest after the unit on elections.

A control group consisting of one class of twenty-three eighth grade civics students taught by the author was randomly selected. This control group was exposed to a unit on elections consisting of traditional methods of lecture, worksheets, and textbook assignments, but not exposed to the constructivist use of technology. The remaining five sections of students were exposed to a unit consisting of the same traditional methods as the control group for half of the unit, but were then exposed to constructivist use of technology for the other half of the unit. At the conclusion of the unit, the control group showed no increase from pretest to posttest. However, for the experimental group, after having produced a public service announcement for both radio and television, a clear increase was documented. For example, when asked on the pretest whether they felt that they could have an influence on the decisions made in their community (with a response of 1 indicating "not at all" and 5 indicating "totally agree"), the experimental group's average response went from a pretest score of 3 to an average posttest score of 3.8. When asked on the pretest whether they felt that people should try to influence decisions made in a community even if immediate results would not be witnessed, the experimental group's response went from an average pretest score of 3.5 to an average posttest score of 3.9. ... Action research has provided tentative support that technology use may be effective in increasing democratic values of eighth grade students.

Figure 7.3 Sample methodology from an action-research project

action research and frequently is used to do a more formal assessment of products and processes studied and developed through action research (Charles and Mertler, 2002). As a result, action research and evaluation research in many instances are used to study the same topics. However, while action research may simply describe the benefits of a product, process, or approach in order to inform the school community, the purpose of evaluation research is to reach conclusions that will effect decision-making. Action research is generally localized to the school building while evaluation research may look at a specific program and evaluate its effects on an entire district or beyond. The Tennessee Project STAR study which was described at the beginning of this chapter is an example of a large-scale evaluation involving many schools across an entire state.

There are two categories of evaluation research: formative and summative. Formative evaluation research is conducted while an activity, process, or system is still being developed in order to make decisions to improve its effectiveness. It is frequently integrated with an action-research project. Summative evaluation is conducted to reach a decision about the effectiveness of an activity, process, or approach after development. Of the two, summative evaluation is more common.

Process and procedures in evaluation research
The process and procedures used in evaluation research are similar to those used in action research. A wide range of educational topics (products, processes, approaches) are appropriate foci for evaluation research. Evaluation research may either be school-based or extend beyond schools and focus on particular activities across a school district. Because of this expansion in scope, evaluation research tends to rely on quantitative data-collection techniques. Evaluation research is very popular for doing cost-benefit studies, especially of government and other grant-funded programs. Examples of topics appropriate for evaluation research include:

- the effectiveness of a new textbook series
- a cost-benefit analysis of a statewide initiative to integrate technology across the curriculum
- the effectiveness of an extended school day program on student achievement.

Research questions (see Figure 7.4) are more common than hypotheses. Examples include:

What has been the effect of an extended-day program on student achievement in the Metro School District?
What are the cost-benefits of implementing an all-day prekindergarten program in the Ringwood School District?
What have been the effects of the new _____ textbook series on student performance amongst high-school students in Gotham City?

Hypotheses may be used depending upon the research methodologies and designs used.

Purpose	The purpose of evaluation research is to make a determination or judgment on the merits of product, process, or approach.
Hypothesis/Research questions	Research questions are more frequently used instead of hypotheses. They are stated broadly and usually early on as part of the research planning process.
Data collection/Sources	Primarily quantitative data is collected although some qualitative techniques can also be used. School records, surveys, and questionnaires are common sources.
Data analysis	Quantitative data can be analyzed using a computer software program such as SPSS, usually to conduct simple descriptive analysis (e.g., frequency distributions, means, standard deviations). Depending upon the design of the study, more sophisticated statistical analyses can be conducted.
Reporting results	The format of these reports are frequently less formal and do not always follow a rigid research report format. Sometimes evaluation researchers wish to share their work with a larger professional community and will publish reports of their findings in journals. In these cases, the reports should be more formally organized. Most evaluation studies are not meant to be generalized to larger populations, however, some suggest that products or processes that have been determined to be successful should be adopted by other schools or districts.

Figure 7.4 Planning for evaluation research

Data collection for evaluation research relies on quantitative techniques more than qualitative techniques, however, both can be used. Student records, performance data, surveys, and questionnaires are common sources of data. These can be followed up with interviews and other qualitative data-collection techniques. Quantitative data should be converted to electronic form and analyzed using a statistical software package. A range of statistical techniques can be applied depending upon the research design.

Report presentations do not necessarily follow a strict research-report format. Reports that will be used within a local school district can be brief and to the point. Reports that might be published or submitted to a funding agency may be more formalized. If a longer format is used, an executive summary is frequently included at the beginning of the report. Some funding agencies may provide their own report formats. Consistency of quantitative presentations (e.g., tables, graphs, statistical findings) is always considered good report design.

Figures 7.5 and 7.6 are excerpts from two evaluation research projects. In Figure 7.5, the excerpt is from a project entitled "Age 21 cost-benefit analysis of the Title I Chicago Child-Parent Centers" by Arthur J. Reynolds, Judy A. Temple, Dylan L. Robertson, and Emily A. Mann, and is an extensive longitudinal study of the cost-benefits of Child-Parent Centers in Chicago. The excerpt provides a brief description of the methodology as well as a policy statement recommending expansion of this type of program. Figure 7.6 is an excerpt from a formative evaluation research project entitled "New Jersey school nurses' perceptions of school-based, prenatal nutrition education" by Bernadette Garchinsky Janas and Jacqueline Kay

---

This excerpt is taken from an article entitled "Age 21 cost-benefit analysis of the Title I Chicago Child-Parent Centers" by Arthur J. Reynolds, Judy A. Temple, Dylan L. Robertson, and Emily A. Mann. It was published in *Educational Evaluation & Policy Analysis*, **24**(4): 267–303, Winter 2002. The entire article is available on the Internet from Wilson Web (Education) Full Text Services.

SAMPLE AND DESIGN
The Chicago Longitudinal Study (CLS, 1999) investigates the life-course development of 1,539 children from low-income families; 93% are black and 7% are Hispanic. Born in 1980, children and families in this ongoing study attended kindergarten programs in 25 sites in 1985–86 (Reynolds, 1999, 2000). The original sample included the entire cohort of 989 children who completed preschool and kindergarten in all 20 Child-Parent Centers with combined programs and 550 low-income children who did not attend the program in preschool but instead participated in a full-day kindergarten program in five randomly selected schools and in schools affiliated with the Child-Parent Centers. 14.8 percent of the comparison group attended Head Start preschool; the remaining children were in home care . . .

POLICY IMPLICATIONS
Findings of the study support the value of investments in high-quality interventions for low-income children. Since nearly one-half of all eligible children do not enroll in center-based early care and education programs (National Center for Educational Statistics, 2002) and the quality of services that many receive is not high (U.S. General Accounting Office, 1999), programs with demonstrative effectiveness like the Child-Parent Centers warrant expansion.

Figure 7.5 Sample methodology and conclusion from an evaluation research project

This excerpt is taken from an article entitled "New Jersey school nurses' perceptions of school-based, prenatal nutrition education" by Bernadette Garchinsky Janas and Jacqueline Kay Hymans. It was published in *The Journal of School Health*, **67**: 62–7, Fall 1997. The entire article is available on the Internet from Wilson Web (Education) Full Text Services.

The Pregnant Teenagers' Nutrition Education Project (PTNEP) was undertaken to provide more comprehensive and accessible nutrition education services to pregnant adolescents in New Jersey. The PTNEP used *formative evaluation research* (FN24, 25) to identify channels to deliver ongoing dietary guidance to pregnant teens, and to understand barriers associated with these channels. Although the PTNEP did not set out to develop a school-based program per se, the formative evaluation process quickly identified school nurses as accessible and qualified individuals who could provide dietary guidance to pregnant teens throughout the course of pregnancy.

This manuscript reports results from the PTNEP formative evaluation, which consisted of two phases. Phase one involved a focus group and semi-structured interviews with health and social service professionals who work with adolescents. The objectives of phase one were to identify barriers to nutrition education and dietary change among pregnant adolescents, and to develop a plan for a nutrition education program. Phase two, which was based on results from phase one, involved a survey of public high school nurses in New Jersey to assess their interest in, and perceptions of barriers to, providing nutrition education to pregnant adolescents in their schools. Results from this formative research are being used to guide the development and implementation of a school-based, prenatal nutrition education program for pregnant teenagers in the state.

Figure 7.6 Sample methodology of a formative evaluation research project

Hymans. This excerpt summarizes a two-phase formative evaluation research project to improve and develop the Pregnant Teenagers' Nutrition Education Project in New Jersey.

Readers who wish to pursue further information on evaluation research methodology may search ERIC or Wilson Web (Education) Full Text Services, and use keywords "evaluation research."

8

Sharing results: the research report

In 1982, Cynthia Beck, a graduate student, was conducting a study for her masters thesis on burnout among teachers in rural school districts in northern Ohio. Her thesis advisor for this study was Dr. Richard Gargiulo. The study specifically examined burnout among teachers of mildly retarded, moderately retarded, and nonretarded children. She developed a survey instrument that was sent to 997 full-time teachers. The instrument consisted of:

- eight questions on demographic characteristics and occupational responsibilities
- twenty-five statements from the Maslach Burnout Inventory
- ten questions assessing the incidence of stress-related physical symptoms.

She hypothesized that the degree of teacher burnout would significantly increase as the students' level of intellectual functioning decreased. Most educators would have assumed that this hypothesis would be retained.

When the questionnaires were returned and the data analyzed, the major finding was contrary to what she expected. In fact, her data suggested that special education teachers experienced not only fewer but weaker symptoms of burnout. Cynthia completed her thesis and subsequently wrote an article that was published in the *Journal of Educational Research* (1983). In this article, co-authored with Dr. Gargiulo, she reported the results of her study and speculated on why the findings were contrary to what she expected. Perhaps smaller class sizes in special education eased stress and burnout, or personality differences exist in teachers who choose to work with special education children, or that special education teachers because of their training were prepared to expect smaller successes with their students. This article provided important new knowledge and added to our understanding of burnout and stress among teachers. Twenty years later it was still being cited for its contribution (see Stempien and Loeb, 2002).

THE RESEARCH REPORT

The seeking and building of knowledge is important for the educational community as well as for the individual researcher. Even if results are contrary to expectations, good research adds to our knowledge base. In this chapter, formats for reporting and sharing results with others in a clear and effective manner are examined. The researcher has several venues for preparing a formal report: thesis, dissertation, journal article, paper presented at a professional conference, or an evaluation report for a funding agency. Unfortunately no single format has been adopted for all of these purposes. Grant and other funding agencies will likely specify a format for an evaluation. Professional societies may limit significantly the length of a paper that will appear in conference proceedings. Theses and dissertations generally follow a particular format. Journal articles follow formats that are similar to theses and dissertations but are expected to be somewhat shorter. This chapter will examine the research-report formats appropriate for journal articles, theses and dissertations, and professional conference papers. In addition, style manuals provide the publication rules (e.g., citations, quotations, reference listings, heading and subheading positioning) for research reports. In education research, the American Psychological Association (APA) *Manual of Style* is the most popular, especially for quantitative studies. The University of Chicago *Manual of Style* is also popular especially for qualitative studies. Readers should consult the newest versions of these manuals for stylistic details.

JOURNAL ARTICLES

One of the more common venues for sharing a study is the professional journal. One of the benefits of doing research in a popular academic field such as education is that there are many journals available for publishing scholarly work. The more respected journals have a publishing review process that requires manuscript submissions to be refereed by other professionals in the field. Generally two or more referees are asked to review a submission and give a recommendation to publish, not to publish, or to revise and resubmit for publication. This is a desirable process that ensures the journal's quality and provides feedback to the writer from someone knowledgable in the field. Generally this review is completely anonymous with neither the submitter or reviewers knowing each other's names. Reviewers are usually authors and experts who have established a publication record with the journal. In addition to reviewing the substance of the study or manuscript, reviewers will examine the format and check for compliance with the established publication style standards of the journal. The guidelines for submitting a manuscript to a journal are almost always available in every edition.

The most common format for submitting a research article is outlined in Figure 8.1. This format follows closely the proposal format described in Chapter 2.

The title page is usually straightforward and researchers should reference the journal's guidelines for style. The title should be clear and contain no superfluous words. In developing a title, the researcher should keep in mind that others may use a keyword search system to locate published materials on a topic. Generally, these keyword systems will use words or phrases in the title as primary entries.

The abstract is a brief summary (never more than one page) of the entire study and should include the statement of purpose and brief summaries of the methodology and findings. The abstract is important because it is generally the first part of the article that will

---

Journal article format

Title

Abstract

Introduction/Statement of the problem

Hypothesis/Research questions

Review of the literature

Methodology/Procedures

Findings/Results

Conclusions/Discussion

References

Appendices

Figure 8.1 Suggested format for a journal article

be read and will determine whether or not the other parts will be read.

The introduction/statement of the problem is meant to establish the importance of the research. Any references from authorities or experts in the field, or statements made by policy-makers or government officials that support the importance, usefulness, or timeliness of the research can be included. The introduction should conclude with a declarative statement of purpose that begins with "The purpose of this study was. ...." The past tense is used because the research has been completed.

Following the introduction, the hypotheses and research questions are stated in the exact wording used to guide the research.

The review of the literature is a critical component of any research report because it helps frame the topic within the research and conclusions of others. In writing the review, the researcher should consider how the study "fits in" with or complements other studies on the same topic. Chapter 2 covers many of the key considerations in developing a review of the literature.

The methodology/procedures section describes the study design. Depending upon the type of research methodology used, the researcher emphasizes different aspects of the design. See chapters on ethnographic, historical, descriptive, correlational, causal-comparative, experimental, action and evaluation research. Generally though a description of setting, subjects, data-collection instruments and sources, statistical procedures and other analyses are provided. In addition, the researcher should provide a rationale for the design. Any control procedures used to ensure the validity of the methodological approaches should be fully presented. Any data-collection instruments that were developed as part of the study should be described and if possible included in an appendix.

As part of the methodology/procedures section, the researcher should also define any key terms that have not been defined earlier in the article. Key terms may be any terms or acronyms (e.g., IEP – Individual Evaluation Plan, SLT – School Leadership Teams, SBM – School-Based Management) that have a specific technical meaning. Key terms also include commonly used terms that have a specific definition in the proposal such as "academic achievement as defined by student scores on a [specific] standardized test."

The findings/results is considered by many the most important section of any research report. The researcher should describe as completely and as clearly as possible the results obtained from the analyses described in the methodology. Data (tables, graphs, figures) that support the findings should be presented in a consistent format. The text should explain any tables or graphs which may need interpretation. The researcher should not assume that the reader will understand the statistical procedures used. A very brief review is helpful but, by the same token, a complete tutorial on the statistics used should not be provided.

The conclusion/discussion section should relate the results to the hypotheses or research questions stated at the beginning of the study. The researcher should clearly state whether the hypotheses were retained or not. If research questions were used, then the researcher should provide the answers as directly as possible. If the findings were not as expected (assuming there are no methodological flaws), they still are important and the researcher is free to provide informed comments or speculations.

The researcher should be careful, perhaps even modest, in presenting findings. Most research in education and the social sciences adds incrementally to what is known. The researcher should carefully fit the findings into the research literature that was presented in the review of the literature section. Do the findings support or refute earlier research? Does the researcher have suggestions for future research projects on the same topic? The researcher may also comment on any implications for educational practice or policy that might derive from the findings.

The report concludes with a list of references and any appendices. The researcher again should refer to the stylistic guidelines provided by the journal for these sections.

Generally, the editor of a journal will specify suggested lengths for articles in the publication guidelines and these will help guide the researcher's writing. If the researcher feels limited by the length restrictions, the editor may be contacted to determine if he or she will make any exceptions. If not, the researcher may wish to submit the article to another journal or attempt to reduce the manuscript to fit within the journal's guidelines. If the latter direction is chosen, the researcher may wish to look especially at the review of the literature section to see if this can be streamlined or reduced.

For further information on publishing a research article, the American Educational Research Association maintains a website entitled "Publishing Educational Research: Guidelines and Tips" at <http://www.aera.net/pubs/howtopub/index.html>.

WRITING A THESIS OR DISSERTATION

Universities establish their own formats for preparing a thesis or dissertation. Usually these are very specific and provide information on all of the stylistic conventions used. However, they generally follow a common format. Figure 8.2 provides a typical format that is appropriate for most theses and dissertations submitted in the field of education. There are many similarities between the way a journal article and a thesis are presented as will be seen in this chapter.

The title page and front matter are relatively straightforward and the researcher should reference the university's guidelines for preparing these parts of the thesis or dissertation. The title should be clear and stated as directly as possible without any superfluous words. Acknowledgments are made to show appreciation to those

---

Thesis and dissertation format

Title page

Front matter

   Acknowledgments

   Table of contents

   List of tables

   List of figures

Abstract

Chapter I – Introduction

   Statement of the problem

   Hypotheses/Research questions

   Significance of the problem/theoretical framework

   Definition of terms

Chapter II – Review of the literature

Chapter III – Methodology/Procedures

Chapter IV – Findings/Results

Chapter V – Conclusions/Discussion

References

Appendices

Figure 8.2 Report format for a thesis or dissertation

who have helped the researcher in his or her studies. Usually there are a number of family, friends, and mentors who have provided assistance. Lists of tables and figures are standard practice and should be included in the front matter.

The abstract is important because it is generally the first part of the thesis or dissertation that will be read and will determine whether or not the other parts will be read. Within the academic world, very few theses are read in their entirety by others. However, abstracts and selected sections are frequently read and reviewed.

Chapter I introduces the reader to the thesis or dissertation and states why the research was undertaken, its importance, and the expected outcomes. Chapter I should include:

1. Statement of the problem
2. Hypotheses/Research questions
3. Significance of the problem/Theoretical framework – expands on the importance of the problem and should place it within a theoretical framework in education, organization theory, psychology, sociology, or other discipline.
4. Definition of terms.

The above, with the exception of the Significance of the problem/ theoretical framework, are similar in emphasis to a journal article.

Chapter II contains a review of the literature. In a thesis or dissertation, the review is expected to show that the researcher has covered the material in depth and understands the context of the topic or problem. It is frequently lengthy and requires many days of reading, reviewing, and writing. In addition to identifying other major research on the topic, a good review will attempt to provide a synthesis of the literature and demonstrate where the current research might fit.

Chapter III provides a complete description of the methods used to conduct the research. The researcher should provide as much material as necessary to explain fully the procedures used to control the research. Most mentors will read and reread this section several times to be sure that the methodology is appropriate and rigorous enough for the research being presented.

Chapter IV provides a complete presentation of the findings and results of the research. This chapter, in addition to the abstract, is the most likely part of a thesis or dissertation to be read by someone not associated with the research project. It should be comprehensive and include all aspects of what the researcher has found.

Chapter V is the conclusion/discussion of the thesis or dissertation. It should include a summary of the findings in relation to the stated hypotheses or research questions. Any practical implications of the research are also appropriately discussed here. It concludes with recommendations for future study and research on the topic.

References and appendices complete the thesis or dissertation.

CONFERENCE PAPERS AND PRESENTATIONS

Professional conferences abound in education and as a result are the most easily accessible venues for sharing one's research. International, national, and regional conferences are held annually and presenters are sought to share current research. Professional journals and magazines routinely provide calls for papers and presentations for upcoming conferences. Usually these calls are six to eight months in advance of the conference and include contact information and conference websites that provide guidelines for submitting proposals.

Depending on the conference, presentations are sometimes submitted as papers that are published in proceedings or special editions of a journal affiliated to the conference organizers. The guidelines provide the necessary information for submitting a presentation proposal and/or paper that will be published. The format discussed earlier for a journal article is an acceptable format, however, because of limitations on presentation time or length within the proceedings, a manuscript used as a journal article may have to be reduced. In such circumstances the review of the literature is a good place to start. This is usually a lengthy part of an article and audiences at a presentation would rather know more about the methodology and findings than the prior research.

In preparing a proposal for a conference presentation, be sure to follow all guidelines carefully. Increasingly, presentations at conferences rely on multimedia technology using presentation software such as Microsoft's PowerPoint. If the presenter does not know how to use this software, preparing for a conference presentation is a good time to learn. While ultimately the substance of the research is most important, presentation software tools are effective in communicating complex information, especially quantitative-based tables, graphs, and charts, and therefore are highly recommended.

A BRIEF WORD ABOUT WRITING STYLE

It is beyond the scope of this primer to discuss how one should write; however, a few brief comments are in order. First, every researcher should have one or two guidebooks to help develop or refine a style of writing. Strunk and White's *Elements of Style* can be found on this writer's bookshelf with pages well turned and marked. It is one of the most helpful books ever written on the subject of writing. *Elements of Style* has dozens of worthwhile tips to help the researcher write in a clear direct manner and is grounded in the belief that simple declarative sentences are more effective than complex superfluous ones.

Second, the researcher should keep in mind that readers may know little about the study and it is imperative to make sure that all the information necessary for understanding has been provided. This may seem obvious, but after weeks and months working on a study, many details become second nature and might be assumed by the researcher. In writing a report, the researcher should be careful that he or she has not inadvertently omitted details which are important to understanding the material presented. One way to edit for this is to provide a draft of the manuscript to someone who is unfamiliar with the topic. Ask for their suggestions and comments on the manuscript, and particularly whether any parts need clarifications.

Lastly, the researcher should write as honestly and as objectively as possible. Ethics should be paramount to the serious researcher. Every week in both the popular and the professional media, unfounded claims are made that a product or approach will greatly cure, improve, or eliminate this, that, or the other. Claims of this type have no place in education since the molding of children's lives intellectually, socially, and morally is one of the most important and complex of all human endeavors. Praiseworthy educational research is expected to add small bits and pieces to our understanding of the phenomenon rather than provide an all-encompassing solution.

Appendix – A review of statistical procedures

SECTION I – INTRODUCTION

A comprehensive study of statistics is an undertaking that requires extensive time and commitment. However, if one were to scan the educational-research literature, a relatively small number of statistical procedures are used on a regular basis. The purpose of this appendix is to review these procedures and the basic concepts needed to understand how to use and interpret their results. Many educators are not comfortable using statistical procedures to analyze data simply because they do not use them enough to become familiar with their forms, processes, and capabilities. Nevertheless, they are basic tools of measurement, evaluation, and research needed for understanding numerical data.

To begin this review, consider the following numbers:

80, 45, 60, 80, 90, 95, 70.

These numbers have no meaning without the knowledge that they are the scores of seven middle-school students on a social studies test. An educator then might sort them as:

45, 60, 70, 80, 80, 90, 95.

The additional knowledge that the passing score was 70, for example, provides more understanding about this group of numbers; two students failed and five students passed. A quick pencil calculation would show that the average score was 74.28. Suppose, however, that the scores for all middle-school students (N = 1,967) in a selected school district were provided. More complex procedures for organizing, summarizing, and analyzing these numbers would be needed to provide understanding. A listing of the 1,967 scores might be a start but actually would not prove to be very helpful.

Statistical procedures such as frequency distributions, contingency tables (cross-tabulations), means, standard deviations, and correlations could be used to give meaning to the numbers. Indeed, one might even venture to say that it would be impossible to give meaning to them without the assistance of these procedures.

Definitions and key terms
Statistics is a body of mathematical techniques or processes for gathering, organizing, analyzing, and interpreting numerical data. They are basic tools of measurement, evaluation, and research.

The following key terms are part of the basic language of quantitative methods and statistical procedures. Every researcher should be familiar with them.

- **Case, subject** or **observation** – person, place, or thing which is the object of the research. In educational research, it frequently involves students, teachers, classes, schools, parents, or administrators.
- **Variable** or **data element** – an item of data which is collected for each case in the study, and which can vary or have more than one value. Common variables collected in educational research are gender, ethnicity, year of birth, and test scores. Variables can be described as continuous or categorical depending upon how many values they can contain. A continuous variable can contain a wide range of values such as is the case with family income or a test score. A categorical (also referred to as a discrete) variable contains a limited number of values such as in a gender or ethnicity code.
- **Value** – each individual piece of information (e.g., a code, score, response to a question, etc.) for each variable in a study. For example, frequent values for the variable "Gender" are "F" or "M" (also coded as 1 or 2) which represent female and male respectively.
- **Record** or **data record** – a collection of variables or data elements.
- **File** or **data file** – a collection of data records.
- **Scales of measurement** – assignment of numbers to data to help categorize, organize, and interpret them. There are four types of measurement scales:
  1. **nominal scale** – numbers represent categories or classifications such as gender codes, ethnicity codes, etc.
  2. **ordinal scale** – numbers represent rank order such as a ranking of students in a class by grade-point average.

3. **interval scale** – similar to ordinal scale and, in addition, numbers represent equal intervals between each number such as most standardized test scores.

4. **ratio scale** – similar to ordinal and interval scales, and, in addition, has an absolute zero so that numbers can be compared by ratios such as one number being two times or three times larger than another number.

- **Statistical significance (Sig.)** – an indication of the probability of a finding having occurred by chance. It has nothing to do with importance but is simply an indication of probability. Researchers have adopted a general standard referred to as the .05 level of statistical significance, meaning that a finding has a five percent (.05) chance of not being true, or conversely a 95 percent chance of being true. Statistical significance is used in many procedures. For example, in a Oneway Analysis of Variance (ANOVA) procedure trying to determine if there is a statistically significant difference between the mean scores of girls and boys on a fourth-grade standardized reading test. If the results of the Oneway ANOVA showed a statistical significance level of .02, this would mean that the difference in the mean scores has a 98 percent chance of being true and would therefore be statistically significant.

- **Two-tailed v. one-tailed test of significance** – two-tailed and one-tailed tests are probability procedures used in testing hypotheses. The term "tailed" refers to the outer fringes or "tails" of the normal distribution curve. A two-tailed test assumes that the hypothesis is nondirectional. An example of a nondirectional hypothesis is: "There is no difference in computer literacy between newly hired and experienced teachers." A one-tailed test assumes that the hypothesis is directional. An example of a directional hypothesis is: "Newly hired teachers are more computer literate than experienced teachers." Once a hypothesis is stated in such a way that one group is assumed to be greater, lesser, higher, etc., it is considered a directional hypothesis. Of the two types of tests, the two-tailed test is more commonly used.

- **Standard error** – a statistical inference that assumes that the true measure (e.g., mean, correlation, difference of means) lies within a stipulated range above and below the actual value calculated for the measure. For example, the standard error for a mean of 88.5 may be 1.4 plus or minus from the mean. A researcher could then state with a great deal of confidence that the true mean for the population is between 87.1 and 89.9. The low-end (e.g, 87.1) and high-end (e.g, 89.9) of the standard error from the mean are referred to as the confidence limits and the range between the low and high is referred to as the confidence interval. A general rule is that the smaller the standard error, the more reliable is the calculated value.

- **Degrees of freedom** – a mathematical concept which indicates the number of observations or values in a distribution that are independent of each other or are free to vary. They are used with various measures to refine the results of treatments of probability or chance. For example, in a distribution of three numbers which can vary but the sum of which has to equal 100, although three separate numbers can be selected, in reality, only two numbers need be selected because the third number would be determined by the first two numbers. More precisely, if 30 and 50 are selected, the third number has to be 20. The numbers 30 and 50 are independent but 20 is dependent on the first two numbers. In this example, there are two independent values or two degrees of freedom. Calculating the degrees of freedom for many statistical measures can be time-consuming and complex. Fortunately, most statistical computer software packages calculate degrees of freedom automatically. The abbreviation for degrees of freedom is "DF" and appears routinely on many statistical reports.

Types of data
In the application of statistical treatments, two types of data are recognized:

- **parametric data** – data which are measured and which are assumed to be normally or near normally distributed. Examples include most standardized tests such as I.Q. tests, SAT, and GRE.
- **nonparametric data** – data which are distribution free, and which are generally counted or ranked. Examples include demographic data such as gender or ethnicity; and categorized data such as pass/fail and responses such as yes/no.

Types of analysis
In the application of statistical treatments, two types of analysis are recognized:

- **descriptive analysis** – limits generalizations or conclusions, based on statistical analysis, to the particular group of individuals or cases observed. No attempt is made to extend these generalizations or conclusions beyond the observed group.

- **inferential analysis** – draws conclusions about a larger population based on a smaller sample which is assumed to be representative of the larger population from which it is drawn. An important aspect of inferential analysis is establishing that the smaller sample population is representative of the larger population.

SECTION II – SIMPLE DESCRIPTIVE STATISTICAL PROCEDURES

Several simple descriptive statistical procedures provide the starting point for analyzing numerical data for many research projects. These procedures help the researcher become familiar with the data, identify missing or incorrect data, and provide an introductory description of the data in a research report. While many statistical procedures can be used for these purposes, two of the more popular are frequency distributions and contingency tables (also referred to as cross-tabulations). These procedures can be used with any qualitative or quantitative research methodology where numerical data have been collected. For most research reports, it is considered good style to include basic information about the setting and subjects. Descriptive statistics are an excellent way to provide this information in an efficient and effective manner.

Frequency distributions
A frequency distribution is a systematic arrangement of numeric values from the lowest to the highest or the highest to the lowest – with a count of the number of times each value was obtained. As an example, a group of students completed a standardized mathematics test as part of a study. The results of this test include a performance level indicator as follows:

1 = failed to meet standard
2 = almost met standard/still needs to improve
3 = met standard
4 = excelled in meeting the standard.

It would be possible to write a paragraph describing the student performance on this test, however, a simple frequency distribution table (see Figure A.1) would be just as effective and possibly more so. The SPSS (Statistical Package for the Social Sciences) program commands that generated the Figure A.1 are in the Analyze menu in Descriptive Statistics – Frequencies (see Figure A.2). If this data

Performance level code	Number of students	Percentage
1 = failed to meet standard	16	14.5
2 = almost met standard/still needs to improve	36	32.7
3 = met standard	39	35.5
4 = excelled in meeting the standard	19	17.3
Total	110	100.0

Figure A.1 Sample frequency distribution

A705BOOKMathTestData.sav - SPSS Data Editor

File Edit View Data Transform Analyze Graphs Utilities Window Help

	Name	Type			
			Reports	▶	
			Descriptive Statistics	▶	Frequencies...
1	student	Numeric	Compare Means	▶	Descriptives...
2	grade	Numeric	General Linear Model	▶	Explore...
3	gender	String	Mixed Models	▶	Crosstabs...
4	age	Numeric	Correlate	▶	Ratio...
5	class	Numeric	Regression	▶	
6	yearsps1	Numeric	Loglinear Classify	▶	YearsPS12
7	reason	Numeric	Data Reduction	▶	
8	number	Numeric	Scale	▶	
9	oper	Numeric	Nonparametric Tests	▶	
10	model	Numeric	Survival	▶	
11	meas	Numeric	Multiple Response	▶	
11	meas	Numeric	11	0	
12	stat	Numeric	11	0	
13	pattern	Numeric	11	0	
14	scale_sc	Numeric	11	0	Scale Score
15	plevel	Numeric	11	0	Prf Level
16					

Figure A.2 Screen capture of SPSS commands for generating a frequency distribution

were an important aspect of a study, a barchart could be added to provide a picture of the distribution (see Figure A.3). Generating a barchart is an option in the SPSS Frequencies menu. If appropriate or needed for analysis, SPSS also provides an option to overlay a normal curve on the barchart.

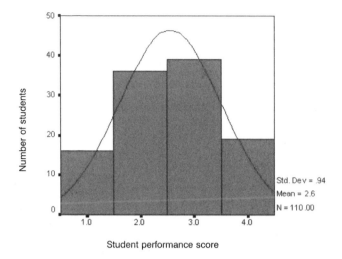

Figure A.3 Sample barchart for a frequency distribution

Frequency distributions can be most useful in helping the researcher to identify missing or incorrect data. In the example in Figure A.1, suppose one or more codes was a 0 or a 5 or any value other than 1, 2, 3 or 4. These would show up on the frequency distribution table. The researcher would know that there were errors in the data and could take steps to correct them. In the initial data analysis stages, frequency distributions should be generated for all key variables to identify any data entry errors or missing data.

Contingency tables (cross-tabulations)
Suppose after generating the frequency distribution in the example in Figure A.1, the researcher wanted to compare the results of boys with those of girls. One simple approach would be to generate two frequency distributions (one for boys and one for girls) and line them up side by side. An even simpler approach would be to do a contingency table, also called a cross-tabulation. A contingency table is an arrangement of data in a two-dimensional classification scheme represented by a series of rows and columns. Figure A.4 is a contingency table showing the frequencies and percentages of student performance levels by gender. The table is arranged with the data for gender in the columns and data for performance level in the rows. The SPSS program commands that generated the example in Figure A.4 are in the Analyze menu in Descriptive

Performance level* GENDER crosstabulation

			GENDER		
			Female	Male	Total
Performance level	Failed to meet standard	Count	11	5	16
		% within performance level	68.8%	31.2%	100.0%
		% within GENDER	18.6%	9.8%	14.5%
	Almost met standard/ Still needs improvement	Count	22	14	36
		% within performance level	61.1%	38.9%	100.0%
		% within GENDER	37.3%	27.5%	32.7%
	Met standard	Count	15	24	39
		% within performance level	38.5%	61.5%	100.0%
		% within GENDER	25.4%	47.1%	35.5%
	Excelled in meeting standard	Count	11	8	19
		% within performance level	57.9%	42.1%	100.0%
		% within GENDER	18.6%	15.7%	17.3%
Total		Count	59	51	110
		% within performance level	53.6%	46.4%	100.0%
		% within GENDER	100.0%	100.0%	100.0%

Figure A.4 Sample contingency table (cross-tabulation)

Statistics – Crosstabs (see Figure A.5). Contingency tables are used extensively in research reports to describe data and can be used with any research methodology.

SECTION III – MEASURES OF CENTRAL TENDENCY

Measures of central tendency are among the most popular of all statistical measures. They measure the averages and what is typical for a group of values. The three major measures of central tendency are the mean, median, and mode.

> **Mean** – is the arithmetic average. For example, the mean of the following group of numbers 60, 70, 80, 90, 100 is 80 and is calculated by dividing the sum of the values by the number of values in the group (N = 5): 60+70+80+90+100 = 400/5 = 80

The mean is the most commonly used statistical measure and is most useful in depicting what is typical for a group of values. It is also used extensively within other statistical formulae.

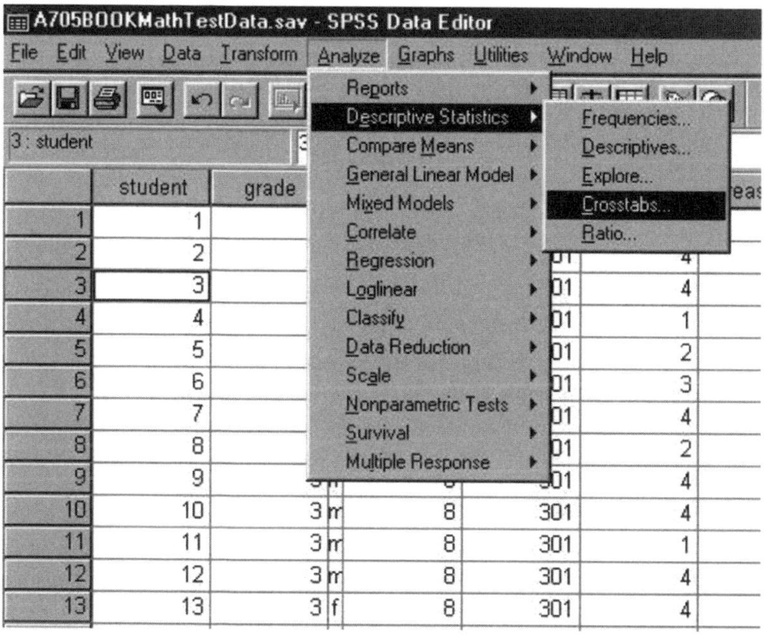

Figure A.5 Screen capture of SPSS commands for generating a cross-tabulation

Median – is the mid-point in a group of values, above and below which one-half of the values fall. In the above example (60, 70, 80, 90, 100), 80 is the median with two scores above and two scores below 80. If there are an even number of values, the median is the point halfway between the two middle values. For example, in the following group of values 70, 70, 80, 82, 90, 100; the median is 81 (halfway between the two middle values 80 and 82).

The median is useful when a few high or very low numbers may distort or skew a mean. For example, the mean for the following annual salaries is $110,400.

$ 10000.
$ 12000.
$ 15000.
$ 15000.
$ 500000.
$ 552000. / 5 = $110400. – calculation for the mean

In this example, the mean is not a good representation of central tendency because there is one very high salary ($500,000.) which is not typical of this group. The median which is $15000. is more typical and a more accurate measure of central tendency in this example. The median is used extensively when presenting data such as salaries, incomes, prices of houses, etc.

Mode – is the value in a group of values which occurs most often. For example, the mode of the following group of numbers 70, 70, 75, 84 is 70.

Of the above measures of central tendency, the mean is the most extensively used in educational research especially in experimental, causal comparative, and quasi-experimental studies. It is used to compare the differences between two or more groups (e.g., pre and posttreatment test, male/female performance indicators, urban/suburban/rural schools). The example that follows shows a comparison of means of three variables from a study conducted in the early 1990s that compared access to technology in schools (N = 136) in two regions. Region I represented large urban school districts and Region II represented nearby suburban school districts. Figure A.6 shows the means of student enrollments in the schools, the means of the number of microcomputers in the schools, and the means of the student per microcomputer ratio. The SPSS program commands that generated the example in Figure A.6 are in the

Comparison of means of student enrollment, number of microcomputers, and student per microcomputer ratio

REGION		Student enrollment	Number of micro- computers per school	Student per micro- computer ratio
Region I – urban	Mean	1344.87	59.58	27.4055
	N	90	90	90
	Std. Deviation	969.500	55.889	11.75778
Region II – suburban	Mean	538.89	49.46	12.6016
	N	46	46	46
	Std. Deviation	265.204	32.666	5.15993
Total	Mean	1072.26	56.15	22.3983
	N	136	136	136
	Std. Deviation	888.583	49.377	12.22424

Figure A.6 Sample comparison of means

	id	re	le					
1	21922P209	1						
2	138071149	1						
3	103RICHMN	1				4	200	0
4	22724P229	1				4	70	33
5	128AMARTN	1				4	150	33
6	173191302	1				1	34	33
7	121MURRO	1				1	160	0
8	20823P327	1				1	28	0
9	21216P309	1				3	24	50
10	125UTRECH	1		3	2600	3	200	0

Figure A.7 Screen capture of SPSS commands for generating a comparison of means

Analyze menu in Compare Means – Means (see Figure A.7). The data show that the mean student enrollment in Region I (urban schools) was much higher than in Region II (suburban schools); that Region I schools had more microcomputers per school than Region II; and that the student per microcomputer ratio was much higher in Region I. The study concluded that while urban schools on average had more technology (microcomputers) due to their much higher enrollments, the students in urban schools actually had less access to technology (students per microcomputer).

t test

The t test is a parametric (assumes normal distribution) test to determine the significance of the difference between the means of two groups of values. The t test uses the mean, the variance, and a table of critical values for a "t" distribution to calculate a "t" value. The rejection or acceptance of the statistical significance of the differences in two means is based on a standard that no more than 5 percent (.05 level) of the difference is due to chance or sampling error, and that the same difference would occur 95 percent of the time should the test be repeated. Some researchers use a more rigorous standard of 1 percent (.01 level), and that the same difference would occur 99 percent of the time should the test be repeated.

The t test usually is displayed in a study or report as follows: the experiment or treatment group (M = 86.50, SD = 4.31) scored significantly higher than the control group (M = 79.10, SD = 5.22), t(80) = 4.90, p<.05 where

M = Mean
SD = Standard Deviation
t = t value
number in parenthesis (80) after the t value = N (number of cases adjusted for degrees of freedom)
p = indicates the level of statistically significant difference (e.g., .05 level) between the two means.

In the above example, p is the value that indicates at what level a statistically significant difference exists.

Figure A.8 shows the results of a t test procedure executed with SPSS. In this figure, the data from the previous example were used, specifically the means of the number of microcomputers per school in Region I were compared with Region II. The data in Figure A.8 show that the t statistic is 1.132 and the p value (Sig.) is .260. Since the p value is greater than .05, there is no statistically significant difference in the means of the number of microcomputers in the schools in the two regions. The SPSS t test procedure includes a feature to determine if the variances of the two groups are equal (F statistic in the Levene test). This is a basic test for determining if the data is normally distributed. In this example, the significance value of the F statistic is .15. Because this value is greater than .10, one can assume that the groups have equal variances and ignore the second test. If the variances were not equal, the F statistic significance value would be .10 or lower, and one would then use the second test. The

Independent samples test

| | | Levene's test for equality of variances | | | | | | |
		F	Sig.	t	df	Sig. (2-tailed)	Mean difference	Std. error difference
Number of micro- computers per school	Equal variances assumed	6.125	.150	1.132	134	.260	10.12	8.940
	Equal variances not assumed			1.330	131.524	.186	10.12	7.609

Figure A.8 Sample t-test procedure comparing the means of the number of microcomputers in Region I and Region II schools

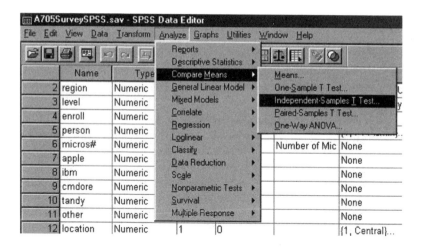

Figure A.9 Screen capture of SPSS commands for generating a t test

SPSS program commands that generated the example in Figure A.8 are in the Analyze menu in Compare Means – Independent Samples T Test (see Figure A.9).

One limitation of a t test is that it can only be used with two groups. For three or more groups, an analysis of variance is the appropriate statistical procedure.

Analysis of variance (ANOVA)

Analysis of variance is a statistical measure used for determining whether differences exist among two or more groups. It does this by comparing the means of the groups to see if they are statistically different. Analysis of variance uses the mean, the variance, and a table of critical values for "F" distribution to calculate an "F" statistic. Analysis of variance is a parametric (assumes normal distribution) test. Statistical significance of the differences in two or more means is based on a standard that no more than 5 percent (.05 Level) of the difference is due to chance or sampling error, and that the same difference would occur 95 percent of the time should the test be repeated.

Analysis of variance can be used for several different types of analyses.

- **Oneway analysis of variance** – assumes there are two variables with one variable a dependent, interval, or ratio variable (numerical data that show quantity and direction), and one variable, an independent nominal variable or factor such as an ethnicity code or sex code.

- **N-way analysis of variance** – assumes there are three or more variables with one variable a dependent, interval or ratio variable and two or more, independent, nominal variables or factors such as ethnicity code or sex code.
- **Multiple regression** – assumes there are three or more variables with one variable a dependent, interval or ratio variable and two or more, independent, interval or ratio variables such as test scores, income, grade-point average, etc.
- **Analysis of covariance** – assumes there are three or more variables with one variable a dependent, interval or ratio variable and two or more variables are a combination of independent, nominal, interval or ratio variables.

Depending on the options used, ANOVA can be presented in different ways in a study or a report. The simplest form of an analysis of variance is the Oneway ANOVA as follows. The analysis of variance indicated that there were significant differences among the four groups F (3,96) = 7.50, p<.01 where

F = the F statistic
the two numbers in parentheses (3,96) = the number of groups and N (number of cases adjusted for degrees of freedom)
p = the level of statistically significant difference (e.g., 01 level) among the means.

In the above example, p is the value that indicates at what level a statistically significant difference exists.

Another popular way of presenting a Oneway ANOVA is as a table as illustrated in Figure A.10 which shows the results of a Oneway ANOVA that was performed on the access to technology data introduced earlier. The Oneway procedure was performed

Student per microcomputer ratio

	Sum of squares	df	Mean square	F	Sig.
Between groups	6671.362	1	6671.362	66.210	.000
Within groups	13501.953	134	100.761		
Total	20173.315	135			

Figure A.10 Sample Oneway ANOVA procedure using student per microcomputer ratio as the dependent variable and region as the independent variable

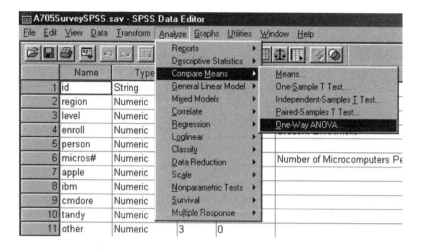

Figure A.11 Screen capture of SPSS commands for generating a oneway analysis of variance

with one independent variable (region) and one dependent variable (student per microcomputer ratio). The final column (Sig. = .000) is the statistical significance of the differences in the means and indicates that there is a statistically significant difference between the means in the two regions for the student per microcomputer ratio. The SPSS program commands that generated the above example are in the Analyze menu in Compare Means – Oneway ANOVA (see Figure A.11).

Figure A.12 shows the results of a Oneway ANOVA that was used for more than two groups. The Oneway procedure was performed with one independent variable (level) and one dependent variable (student per microcomputer ratio). Level refers to three school groups (primary, middle, secondary). The final column (Sig. = .003) is the statistical significance of the differences in the

Student per microcomputer ratio

	Sum of squares	df	Mean square	F	Sig.
Between groups	1709.472	2	854.736	6.157	.003
Within groups	18463.844	133	138.826		
Total	20173.315	135			

Figure A.12 sample Oneway ANOVA procedure using student per microcomputer ratio as the dependent variable and level as the independent variable

N-way Anova[a,b]

			Sum of squares	df	Mean square	F	Sig.
Student per microcomputer	Main effects	Combined	2099.352	5	419.870	3.134	.011
		LEVEL	1380.262	2	690.131	5.152	.007
		PERSON	174.968	3	58.323	.435	.728
	2-way interaction	LEVEL*PERSON	1174.358	6	195.726	1.461	.197
	Model		3631.822	11	330.166	2.465	.008
	Residual		16477.166	123	133.961		
	Total		20108.988	134	150.067		

a. Student per microcomputer ratio by LEVEL, PERSON
b. All effects entered simultaneously

Figure A.13 Sample N-way ANOVA procedure using student per microcomputer ratio as the dependent variable and level and PERSON as the independent variables

means and indicates that there is a statistically significant difference among the means in the three levels for the student per micro-computer ratio.

In executing the Oneway ANOVA procedure for more than two groups, the researcher can perform what is known as a post hoc analysis to determine which of the groups are statistically the most different. The Scheffe test, Fisher's LSD test, and Tukey's HSD test are commonly used for this purpose.

The ANOVA procedure also can be used to examine the effect (difference in means) of more than one independent variable on a dependent variable. Figure A.13 is the output of an N-way ANOVA procedure to determine if there is a difference in the means of the number of students per microcomputer for the two independent variables of level (primary, middle, secondary) and person (administrator, teacher, computer coordinator) responsible for coordinating educational computing.

Before examining the F statistics for the main effect variables (level and person), it is important first to examine the F statistics for the 2-way interaction variables to determine if one of these variables is having a statistically significant effect on the other. This is determined by looking at the F statistic (1.461) and the (Sig. = .197) for the 2-way interactions of level and person. Because the statistical significance is above .05, one can assume that no significant inter-action exists and can proceed to examine the main effects. In other words, the effect of level on students per microcomputer ratios is the same regardless of the person coordinating educational com-puting and the effect of person on students per microcomputer ratios is the same regardless of the level of the school. The combined main effects show an F statistic of 3.134 that is statistically significant (Sig. = .011). The main effect F statistics also indicate that a significant difference exists for level (F = 5.152, Sig. = .007) but that no significant difference exists for person (F = .425, Sig. = .768). In sum, the level of the school has an effect on students per microcomputer ratios but the position of the person responsible for educational computing does not.

Measures of central tendency, especially analysis of means as conducted with t tests and ANOVAs, can be used with a number of different research methodologies and are critical to any study looking to compare two or more groups.

SECTION IV – MEASURES OF DISPERSION

Many educators and researchers rightfully place a good deal of importance on means and measures of central tendency when doing quantitative analysis. However, it can be argued that measures that show how a group of numbers spread or disperse are just as important. Measures of dispersion (also known as measures of spread or variability) show contrasts or differences in a group of values. The major measures of dispersion are the range, deviation, variance, and standard deviation.

- **Range** – is the difference between the highest and lowest values in a group of values. For example, the range of the following group of values 60, 70, 80, 90, 100 is 40 and is calculated by subtracting the lowest value (60) from the highest value (100) = 40. The range is the simplest measure of dispersion and is useful in making an initial determination of the spread in a group of values.
- **Deviation** – is the difference (plus or minus) between a value and the mean of a group of values. For example, if we look again at the group of values used above (60, 70, 80, 90, 100), the deviation of the value 90 in the above group of values is 10, and is calculated by subtracting the mean (80) from the value (90). The deviation is used to determine the distance of one score from the mean.
- **Variance** – is the sum of all the squared deviations from the mean divided by the number (N) of values in the group. In groups of values with an N less than 15, a statistical adjustment is made: the variance is the sum of all the squared deviations from the mean divided by N -1. For example, the variance of the

group of five values 60, 70, 80, 90, 100 is 250 and is calculated as follows:

deviation of 60 from the mean (80) = -20 × -20 = 400
deviation of 70 from the mean (80) = -10 × -10 = 100
deviation of 80 from the mean (80) = 0 × 0 = 0
deviation of 90 from the mean (80) = +10 × +10 = 100
deviation of 100 from the mean (80) = +20 × +20 = 400

Sum of the squared deviations (400 + 100 + 0 + 100 + 400 = 1000) and dividing by 4 (N − 1) = 1000/4 = 250.

The variance is used frequently in a variety of statistical formulae (t test, ANOVA). However, because the deviations are squared, its value is too large in relation to the values in the group to be used as a descriptive measure.

It is difficult, for example, to interpret or determine the meaning of a variance of 250 for the values of 60, 70, 80, 90, 100.

- **Standard deviation** – is the square root of the variance, and the most frequently used measure of dispersion. The standard deviation or S.D. in the above example is 15.811 and is determined by calculating the square root of the variance (250).

As an indication of the importance of these measures of dispersion, the t test and ANOVA procedures described in Section III use the variance to calculate the significance of the differences in the means. In addition, in almost any study where the mean is used to describe a population(s), it is considered good practice to include the standard deviation. As an example of how the standard deviation can provide additional information about a group, consider the means and standard deviations of the following groups of numbers.

Group	A	B	C	D
	70	80	100	100
	70	80	75	100
	70	70	70	70
	70	60	65	40
	70	60	40	40
MEAN (350/5)	70	70	70	70
S.D.	0.0	10.0	21.50	30

The means of the four groups are identical (70) and one might have assumed that the groups are similar. However, these four groups are very different in terms of the degree of dispersion as indicated by the standard deviation. As a matter of fact, the standard deviation describes more accurately the nature of these four groups than does the mean.

Effect size

For t-test and some ANOVA procedures, a secondary statistical procedure called effect size is sometimes used to determine the level of significance in the difference in the means. Effect size is also referred to as a test of practical significance. This can be used, for example, in an experimental study comparing the means of a control group and an experimental group. Effect size is calculated by taking the difference in the means of the two groups and dividing it by the standard deviation of the control group. In education experiments, an effect size of +.20 (20 percent of the standard deviation) would be considered a minimum for sig-nificance; an effect size above +.50 is considered very strong. Some researchers use the effect size (practical significance) in addition to a test of statistical significance. Effect size is also used extensively in meta-analysis where the results of a large number of studies are examined. It is used across all the studies as a common measure of analysis.

Normal distribution (curve)

The normal distribution or curve is based on the standard deviation of a given sample. Many years ago statisticians observed a pattern that when analyzing means and standard deviations for large samples. For example, fundamental data (data not prone to bias or skewness) such as height, weight, or blood pressure, would dis-tribute equally on both sides (plus and minus) of the mean in a "bell-shaped" pattern. Hence, the term "bell-shaped curve." In a normal distribution (see Figure A.14), the distance from one S.D. above the mean to one S.D. below the mean includes approximately 68 percent of all the scores. Plus two to minus two S.D. includes approximately 95 percent of all scores and plus three to minus three S.D. includes over 99 percent of all scores. Many statistical proce-dures including t tests and ANOVAs assume that the groups or populations of analysis are normally or near-normally distributed.

SECTION V – MEASURES OF RELATIVE POSITION

Measures of relative position (also referred to as measures of rela-tive standing) are conversions of values to show where a given value stands in relation to other values of the same grouping. The most common example in education is the conversion of scores on standardized tests to show where a given student stands in relation to other students of the same age, grade level, etc. Converted scores are based on the deviation or distance of a raw score from the mean for a normal curve or distribution. Examples of standard scores used in educational research are: Sigma (z) scores, T scores, SAT/College Board scores, percentiles, and stanines.

- **Sigma (z) score** – the deviation from the mean divided by the standard deviation. It is used to describe a score's deviation from the mean. z scores can have negative as well as positive values. The range is usually -3.00 to +3.00 with a value at the mean of 0.00. For example, a standardized test with a mean of 70 and a standard deviation of 10, a score of 60 would be -10 points from the mean (deviation), divided by the standard deviation (10) equals a z score of -1.00.
- **T score** – a variation of the z score which produces a standard score with a range of 20 to 80 and a mean of 50. It eliminates the decimal and negative z score numbers which are sometimes awkward to work with. The T score is calculated as follows:
    T score = 50 + (10 × Sigma (z) score)
    For example, a z score of -2.00 would have a T score = 50 + (10 × -2.00) or 50 + (-20) or 30.
- **SAT/College Board score** – a variation of the z score which produces a standard score with a range of 200 to 800 and a mean of 500. It is used to spread out the scale. The College Board score is calculated as follows:
    College Board score = 500 + (100 × Sigma (z) score)
    For example, a z score of -2.00 would have a College Board score = 500 + (100 × -2.00) or 500 + (-200) or 300.
- **Percentile** – the point in the distribution below which a given percentage of scores fall. For example, if a score of 65 is at the seventieth percentile then 70 percent of the scores fall below 65.
- **Stanine** – a conversion of raw scores into nine bands or stanines based on the standard deviation, with the fifth stanine containing the mean, the first stanine the lowest scores, and ninth stanine the highest scores.

Figure A.14 illustrates the relationship of the standard scores described above to the normal distribution, the means, and the standard deviation. While measures of relative position can be used in studies involving group analyses, they are particularly effective

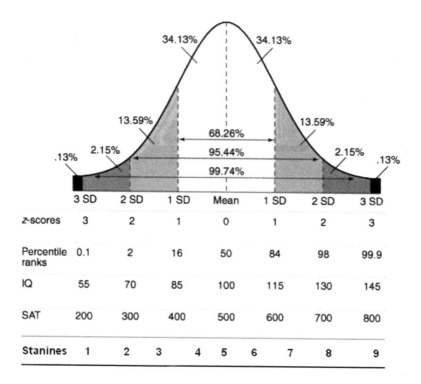

Figure A.14 Normal or bell curve

in studies (e.g., case study) involving a small number of individuals especially where standardized testing is being used.

SECTION VI – MEASURES OF RELATIONSHIP

Measures of relationship examine the relationship between two or more variables or two or more sets of data. They are used extensively in correlational research and can also be used in other methodologies where relationships might be important. Example descriptions of relationships are: there is generally a high positive relationship or correlation between parent's education and academic achievement; there is generally an inverse correlation between the number of microcomputers in a school and the student per microcomputer ratio; and there is generally no relationship or correlation between a person's height and academic achievement. A positive relationship exists when as one variable changes (becomes higher or lower) the other variable changes in the same direction. An inverse relationship exists when as one variable changes, the other variable changes in the opposite direction or as one variable gets higher the other variable gets lower or vice versa. Some forms (e.g., linear regression) of these measures can be used to develop prediction models for determining such things as success in college based on high-school performance. A fundamental aspect of correlational analysis is never to assume that in a relationship a change in one variable *causes* a change in another. Correlational studies focus on relationships and not necessarily cause and effect.

Correlational coefficient

Correlation is the relationship between two variables or sets of data as expressed in the form of a coefficient with +1.00 indicating a perfect positive correlation, -1.00 indicating a perfect inverse correlation, and 0.00 indicating a complete lack of a relationship. Figure A.15 represents the line diagrams for +1.00, -1.00, and 0.00 coefficients. There are several different coefficients which can be produced depending upon the type of variables:

- **Pearson product moment coefficient (r)** is the most popular and is used with two groups of continuous variables (e.g., test scores and grade-point averages).
- **Spearman rank order coefficient (p)** is a form of the Pearson product moment coefficient which can be used with ordinal or ranked data.
- **Phi correlation coefficient** is a form of the Pearson product moment coefficient which can be used with categorical variables (e.g., pass/fail, male/female).

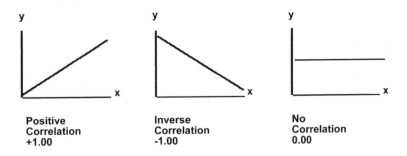

Figure A.15 Line representations of correlation coefficients

There is no simplified method of determining the magnitude of a correlation. Tests of statistical significance can be used but in correlational analysis, very small relationships particularly with large samples will be statistically significant. In fact, if the relationship between two variables is not statistically significant, they will frequently become significant by increasing the N.

Some researchers will use a convention such as follows:

coefficient = .00 to .20 – negligible correlation
coefficient = .21 to .40 – low correlation
coefficient = .41 to .60 – moderate correlation
coefficient = .61 to .80 – substantial correlation
coefficient = .81 to 1.0 – high correlation.

However, these are not uniformly accepted and certain types of studies may establish their own conventions. For example, a correlational study used to establish the reliability of a standardized test might only accept as positive, a coefficient that is higher than .85. Other researchers use a technique whereby they examine the square of the coefficient where r is the coefficient and r^2 is equal to the percent of the variation in one variable that is related to the variation in the other. An r of .5 means 25 percent of the variation in the variables is related since .5 squared equals .25. An r value of .9 means 81 per cent of the variation is related since .9 squared equals .81.

In published studies or reports, correlational coefficients are usually displayed as r values. For example, r = .66, p<.01 where r is the correlational coefficient and p is the level (.01) of statistical significance.

A table or matrix may be used to present correlations especially if many variables are being studied. For example, in Section II of this Appendix, data samples from a study of student performance on a standardized mathematics test were used. Suppose in this data set there were a number of subscores such as reasoning ability, statistical comprehension, and number systems from which an overall main-scale score was calculated. A researcher might want to examine the relationships of each of the subscores to each other as well as to the main-scale score. One simple way to do this would be by generating a correlation matrix (see Figure A.16) of all the subscores and the main-scale score. In examining this matrix, keep in mind that any variable that is correlated to itself will result in a perfect 1.00 coefficient. The researcher might want to consider why the highest relationships exist between the measurement subscore

Correlations

		REASON	NUMBER	OPER	MODEL	MEAS	STAT	PATTERN	Scale score
REASON	Pearson correlation	1	.329**	.378**	.324**	.334**	.321**	.165	.488**
	Sig. (2-tailed)	.	.000	.000	.001	.000	.001	.085	.000
	N	110	110	110	110	110	110	110	110
NUMBER	Pearson correlation	.329**	1	.461**	.532**	.613**	.423**	.156	.724**
	Sig. (2-tailed)	.000	.	.000	.000	.000	.000	.103	.000
	N	110	110	110	110	110	110	110	110
OPER	Pearson correlation	.378**	.461**	1	.400**	.491**	.342**	.158	.618**
	Sig. (2-tailed)	.000	.000	.	.000	.000	.000	.100	.000
	N	110	110	110	110	110	110	110	110
MODEL	Pearson correlation	.324**	.532**	.400**	1	.609**	.397**	.170	.789**
	Sig. (2-tailed)	.001	.000	.000	.	.000	.000	.075	.000
	N	110	110	110	110	110	110	110	110
MEAS	Pearson correlation	.334**	.613**	.491**	.609**	1	.362**	.216*	.734**
	Sig. (2-tailed)	.000	.000	.000	.000	.	.000	.023	.000
	N	110	110	110	110	110	110	110	110
STAT	Pearson correlation	.321**	.423**	.342**	.397**	.362**	1	.127	.555**
	Sig. (2-tailed)	.001	.000	.000	.000	.000	.	.186	.000
	N	110	110	110	110	110	110	110	110
PATTERN	Pearson correlation	.165	.156	.158	.170	.216*	.127	1	.282**
	Sig. (2-tailed)	.085	.103	.100	.075	.023	.186	.	.003
	N	110	110	110	110	110	110	110	110
Scale Score	Pearson correlation	.488**	.724**	.618**	.789**	.734**	.555**	.282**	1
	Sig. (2-tailed)	.000	.000	.000	.000	.000	.000	.003	.
	N	110	110	110	110	110	110	110	110

**Correlation is significant at the 0.01 level (2-tailed).
*Correlation is significant at the 0.05 level (2-tailed).

Figure A.16 Sample correlation matrix

and the number systems subscore (r = .613) or between measurement and modeling (r = .609). Also while all of the subscores correlate with the main-scale score, some correlations (for number systems, measurement, and modeling) are much higher than the others. The SPSS program commands that generated the above example are in the Analyze menu in Correlate – Bivariate (see Figure A.17).

Correlations are frequently represented graphically. Figures A.18 and A.19 illustrate two scattergrams using two correlations from the test score data above in Figure A.16. The first scattergram (A.18) plots the correlation (r =. 789) between the modeling and scale score variables. Because it is such a high correlation, the plot line is almost fully diagonal going from the lower left-hand corner to the upper right-hand corner. The second scattergram (Figure A.19) plots the correlation (r = .282) between the pattern and scale score

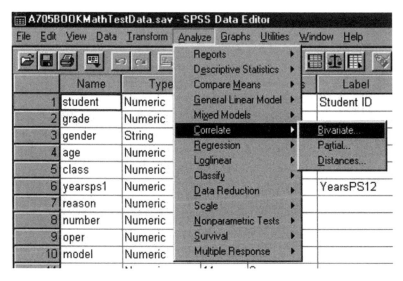

Figure A.17 Screen capture of SPSS commands for generating a correlation matrix

variables. Because it is a weak correlation, the plot line is almost a straight line.

Linear regression and multiple regression
Linear regression is the use of correlation coefficients to plot a line illustrating the linear relationship of two variables X and Y. The correlation coefficient determines the Y intercept and the slope of the line which is represented by the formula: $Y = a + bX$ where

Y = dependent variable
X = independent variable
b = slope of the line
a = constant or Y intercept.

Linear regression is used in making predictions based on finding unknown Y values from known X values. In prediction studies, the Y or dependent variable is frequently referred to as the criterion variable and the X or independent variable is referred to as the predictor variable. An example of a linear-regression formula for predicting college grade-point averages from known high-school grade-point averages would be displayed as follows:

College GPA = a + b (high-school GPA)

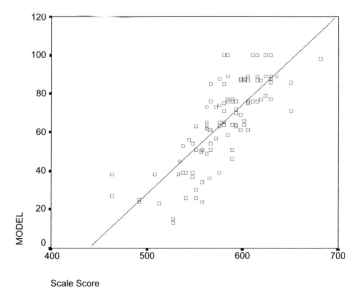

Figure A.18 Sample scattergram illustrating high correlation (.789)

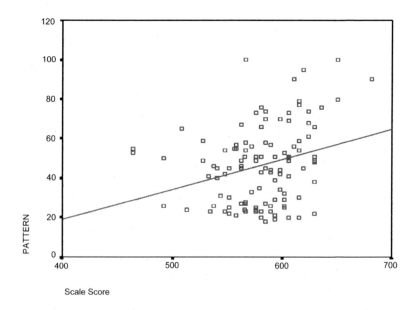

Figure A.19 Sample scattergram illustrating low correlation (.282)

Multiple regression is the same as linear regression except that it attempts to predict Y from two or more independent X variables. The formula for multiple regression is an extension of the linear regression formula:

$$Y = a + b_1 X_1 + b_2 X_2 + \ldots b_N X_N$$

For example, the multiple regression formula for predicting college grade-point average from known high-school grade-point averages and SAT scores would be displayed as follows:

College GPA = $a + b_1$ (high-school GPA) + b_2 (SAT score)

The researcher must be cautious when considering the use of any predictive statistical procedure for educational purposes because many variables influence and affect the people-intensive activities associated with education. It is not always easy to be able to control for them. Predictive studies can provide direction and estimates but should be used carefully in any major decision-making activity.

Before concluding this section on linear and multiple regression, two other procedures should be mentioned.

- **Discriminant analysis** is analogous to multiple regression, except that the independent or criterion variable consists of two categories rather than a continuous range of values.
- **Factor analysis** is used when a large number of correlations have been explored in a given study. It is a means of grouping into clusters or factors certain variables that are moderately to highly correlated.

Reliability and validity of standardized tests
Standardized tests have been used for decades in many countries. They are usually developed by experts and are generally well constructed. Individual test items are analyzed and revised until they meet standards of quality. Objectivity is the goal of most standardized tests, that is, they should not be biased against individuals based on their traits. In addition standardized tests are expected to be reliable and valid. Reliability refers to consistency of results. Validity refers to what a test measures and for whom it is appropriate. Examples of standardized tests include the SAT, GRE, Degrees of Reading Power, and Piers-Harris.

Correlation coefficients are used extensively to measure reliability (consistency of results) and validity (measures what it is supposed to measure) of standardized tests. Simple reliability tests usually involve giving the same test to the same sample of subjects two or more times and then comparing results using correlations which would be expected to be very high. Another approach involves having the same sample of subjects take different questions of the same test (i.e. odd-numbered questions versus even-numbered questions) and compare results using correlation coefficients. Booklets that accompany standardized tests will generally refer to or identify their reliability coefficients.

Validity tests for content of subject matter can be done by a panel of experts and by using statistical analyses. For content validity, panels of experts review questions and attest to their appropriateness. Validity tests for making predictions, such as the use of SAT scores to predict college GPA, usually use correlation coefficients of the two measures (e.g., SAT and GPA) to establish their predictive validity. In establishing reliability and validity of standardized tests, very high correlations (e.g., + .80 and above) are generally expected.

SECTION VII – NONPARAMETRIC ANALYSIS

Many of the statistical procedures discussed thus far in this appendix assumed that the data used were parametric, that is, data which are measured and normally or near-normally distributed. Examples of parametric data include grade-point averages and scores on standardized tests such as SAT and I.Q. Statistical measures such as t tests, analysis of variance, and regression require that one or more of the variables used be parametric. However, many situations arise in educational research where there is a need to do analyses using nonparametric data, that is, data which are not necessarily measured or normally distributed. Examples of nonparametric data include data that are categorized or ranked such as gender codes, ethnicity, types of schools, and grade levels. Examples of statistical procedures which use nonparametric data are:

- **Spearman rank order coefficient** – is a form of the Pearson product moment coefficient (measure of relationship) which is used on ordinal or ranked data.
- **Phi correlation coefficient** – is a form of the Pearson product moment correlation coefficient (measure of relationship) which is used on dichotomous (two possibilities) variables such as pass/fail or female/male.
- **Mann-Whitney test** – is a measure used to test whether two

independent samples come from populations having the same distribution. It uses data which can either be on an interval or ordinal scale and in which values can be ranked from lowest to highest. It is similar to the t-test procedure except it does not assume a normal or near-normal distributed population.

* **Chi-square** – is a measure used to compare actual frequencies and percentages to expected frequencies and percentages of categorized or grouped data.

Chi-square
Chi-square is one of the most frequently used nonparametric statistical procedures and appears often in educational research reports, usually with a contingency table (cross-tabulation) where data are categorized or grouped. Essentially, chi-square conducts a "goodness-of-fit" test by comparing the observed frequencies to the expected frequencies within each category (or cell of a contingency table) to test either that all categories contain the same proportion of values or that each category contains a researcher-specified proportion of values. The result of chi-square is a chi-square statistic that is compared to a table of chi-square values to determine whether the categories (or cell frequencies) are statistically different.

One common application of chi-square is to determine if there is a difference in the proportional representation within samples or comparison groups. For example, if a researcher conducted a national survey of 100 school districts, he or she might want to make sure that different regions (North, South, East, and West) of the country were proportionally represented. Chi-square could make this determination. An earlier reference was made to a survey of access to technology between urban and suburban school districts. Suppose one wanted to determine if the representation of schools by level (primary, middle, secondary) was proportional in the two regions (urban and suburban). Figure A.20 is the output from a chi-square procedure which was executed as an option in an SPSS Crosstabs program to make this determination. The report first displays a "3 by 2" cross-tabulation which shows the count and column percentages of the levels of the schools in this study by region. It is important to know if a difference exists in the distribution of the school levels in order to determine if there is any imbalance (too many or too few schools from any one level) in the way the schools are distributed by region. For example, are there too many high schools in the suburban region, or too few elementary schools? The chi-square summary suggests that there are

LEVEL* REGION Cross-tabulation

			REGION		
			Region I – urban	Region II – suburban	Total
LEVEL	Elementary	Count	50	23	73
		% within REGION	55.6%	50.0%	53.7%
	Middle	Count	22	10	32
		% within REGION	24.4%	21.7%	23.5%
	High	Count	18	13	31
		% within REGION	20.0%	28.3%	22.8%
Total		Count	90	46	136
		% within REGION	100.0%	100.0%	100.0%

Chi-square

	Value	df	Asymp. sig. (2-sided)
Pearson chi-square	1.181[a]	2	.554
Likelihood ratio	1.155	2	.561
Linear-by-linear association	.862	1	.353
N of valid cases	136		

a. 0 cells (.0%) have expected count less than 5. The minimum expected count is 10.49.

Figure A.20 Sample chi-square procedure showing no difference in the cell groupings of categorized data

not. The chi-square statistic (1.181) with 2 degrees of freedom and a significance level of .554 indicates that statistically these groups are similar and no statistical difference exists. Acceptable significance for chi-square is generally at the .05 level. The significance level in this report (.554) is much higher and, therefore, the conclusion is that these groups are not statistically different.

Figure A.21 is the output from another chi-square procedure using the same access to technology data set. The procedure was performed on the variable person which is the position responsible for computer education in the school (e.g., administrator, teacher, coordinator). The purpose of this report is to determine if the schools in the two different regions had different staffing patterns for providing technology education. In the cross-tabulation, the percentages of full-time coordinators (FT COORD) and part-time

PERSON* REGION Cross-tabulation

			REGION		
			Region I – urban	Region II – suburban	Total
PERSON	FT-Admin	Count	29	15	44
		% within REGION	32.2%	32.6%	32.4%
	PT-Tchr	Count	12	5	17
		% within REGION	13.3%	10.9%	12.5%
	FT-Coord	Count	33	6	39
		% within REGION	36.7%	13.0%	28.7%
	PT-Coord	Count	16	20	36
		% within REGION	17.8%	43.5%	26.4%
Total		Count	90	46	136
		% within REGION	100.0%	100.0%	100.0%

Chi-square

	Value	df	Asymp. sig. (2-sided)
Pearson chi-square	13.669[a]	3	.003
Likelihood ratio	14.032	3	.003
Linear-by-linear association	1.589	1	.207
N of valid cases	136		

a. 0 cells (.0%) have expected count less than 5. The minimum expected count is 5.75.

Figure A.21 Sample chi-square procedure showing a difference in the cell groupings of categorized data

coordinators (PT COORD) appear to be different for the two areas. The chi-square summary also suggests that there is a difference. The chi-square statistic (13.669) with 3 degrees of freedom indicates that statistically these groups are different with a significance level of .003 which is lower than the .05 acceptable level of significance.

SECTION VIII – STATISTICAL SOFTWARE PACKAGES

It has been estimated that more than 90 percent of all statistical analysis is performed by computers. The computer can perform statistical calculations more easily, more quickly and more accurately than people using calculators or other devices. Although computers do not make mistakes, people who write programs, collect data, and enter data can and do make them. If poor data are introduced into the computer, the results are likely to contain errors and may be meaningless. Serious researchers have come to see the computer as an invaluable tool and any researcher attempting to do quantitative studies would be wise to take the time to become proficient in using computer technology for collecting data, analyzing them, and reporting the results. Given the proliferation of computer technology in schools and colleges, equipment is generally available with the appropriate statistical software packages so that prospective researchers may practice and learn how to use them.

It is also important that the appropriate software programs needed to support research be selected. Electronic spreadsheet programs such as Excel, Lotus, or Quattro Pro are excellent programs for data collection activities and very simple statistical analysis. The latest version of SPSS has been converted to a spreadsheet-like format so that users familiar with software such as Lotus, Excel, or Quattro Pro can easily learn SPSS. Most of the popular software packages come with their own tutorials, help facilities, and documentation.

For researchers not comfortable with these packages, a workshop or course may be well worth the time and effort. Without developing this expertise, the researcher will be forced to rely on the expertise of others to analyze any substantial amount of quantitative data. Those who do data analysis using statistical packages know that the more familiar and comfortable one is with the data, the more complete and accurate the analysis will be.

Glossary of selected terms used in this primer

This glossary is not meant to be an all-inclusive compilation. It represents some of the important educational research terms and definitions used in this primer. For a more comprehensive glossary on educational research and statistics, readers may wish to refer to the following online resources:

Hyperstat Online
http://davidmlane.com/hyperstat/glossary.html
Statsoft, Incorporated
http://www.statsoftinc.com/textbook/glosfra.html
STEPS – Statistics Glossary
http://www.stats.gla.ac.uk/steps/glossary/index.html

Action research A type of research that studies problems at the local level. It usually focuses on the development, implementation, and testing of a new product, program, plan, or procedure in a school building.

Analysis of variance (ANOVA) A statistical procedure that compares the means of two or more groups to determine if any differences between the means are statistically significant.

Case-study research A type of descriptive research that involves describing and interpreting events, conditions, or situations that are occurring in the present.

Categorical variable A variable, such as gender or ethnicity, that contains a limited number of values. Also referred to as a *discrete variable*.

Causal comparative research A type of research that tries to establish cause-and-effect relationships between two variables where a causal or independent variable cannot be changed or manipulated.

Cause-effect relationship A relationship between two or more variables in which one or more variables affect another variable.

Chi-square A nonparametric test that compares observed frequencies of values of categorical variables to expected values.

CIJE Current Index to Journals in Education.

Confidence interval The true range within which a measure (e.g., mean, correlation) actually lies. The determination of a confidence interval is usually based on the standard error of the measure.

Confidence limits The low and high end of the confidence interval.

Continuous variable A variable such as a test score or salary which contains a wide range or unlimited number of values.

Control group A group of subjects in an experimental study that does not receive the treatment.

Converted score A score that is derived from a raw score and represented in another form that is more easily understood. For example, a percentile ranking is derived from a z score.

Correlation coefficient A decimal number between -1.00 and +1.00 that indicates the degree to which two variables are related.

Correlational research A type of research that uses numerical data to explore the relationship between two or more variables.

Criterion variable In prediction studies, the variable that is predicted by another variable. Also referred to as the dependent variable.

DAI Dissertation Abstracts International.

Degrees of freedom A mathematical concept used with various measures such as t tests, analysis of variance, and chi-square to refine the results of probability or chance in determining statistical significance. It indicates the number of observations or values in a distribution that are independent of each other or are free to vary. Abbrev.: DF.

Dependent variable A variable that changes as a result of or in relation to a change in an independent variable. In prediction studies, it is also referred to as the criterion variable.

Descriptive analysis A data-analysis technique that limits generalizations or conclusions, based on statistical analysis, to the particular group of individuals or cases observed. No attempt is made to extend these generalizations or conclusions beyond the observed group.

Descriptive research A type of research that uses data to describe and interpret events, conditions, or situations that are occurring in the present. It can be qualitative or quantitative depending upon the nature of the data collected.

Deviation The difference (distance plus or minus) between a value and the mean of a group of values.

Dichotomous variable A categorical variable that has only two possibilities (e.g., gender).

Directional hypothesis A hypothesis that states what the researcher expects to find with regard to the direction of the hypothesis testing. For example, "Newly hired teachers are *more* computer literate than experienced teachers."

Discrete variable See *categorical variable*.

Effect size A secondary statistical procedure used to determine the level of significance in the difference in the means. It is calculated by taking the difference in the means of the two groups and dividing it by the standard deviation of the control group.

ERIC Educational Research Information Center.

Ethnographic research A type of descriptive research that involves studying people in their natural or social setting. It is also referred to as "observational research" and "naturalistic inquiry."

Evaluation research A type of research that is done to determine the merits of a product, process, or approach used in education.

Ex post facto research See *causal comparative research*.

Experimental group A group in an experimental study that receives the experimental treatment.

Experimental research A type of research that studies cause (independent variable) and effect (dependent variable) relationships between two or more variables where the causal variable can be manipulated.

External criticism A means of establishing the genuineness of data and providing some proof that data are what they purport to be. Official seals on school records and corroboration of a report through a reliable secondary witness are examples.

External validity The extent to which results can be generalized to larger populations.

Halo Effect A tendency of subjects in an experimental group to exert additional effort because they believe they are part of a special group.

Hawthorne effect A tendency of subjects in an experiment to exert outstanding effort because they know they are part of an experiment.

Historical research A type of descriptive research that involves describing and interpreting events, conditions, or situations that have occurred in the past.

Hypothesis A supposition or tentative conclusion without proof that will be used to guide the research.

Independent variable A variable which, as it changes, causes or relates to a change in another (dependent) variable. In prediction studies, it is also referred to as the predictor variable.

Inferential analysis Data-analysis techniques that draw conclusions about a larger population based on a smaller sample which is assumed to be representative of the larger population.

Internal criticism A means of establishing that data are useful for the research project. For example, in a historical study providing evidence that a document's author had knowledge of an event.

Internal validity The extent to which findings can be interpreted accurately especially with regard to the control of extraneous variables.

John Henry effect The tendency of subjects in a control group to exert additional effort because they know they are in a control group and want to outperform the subjects in the experimental group.

Levene test This is a basic test for determining if the data used in certain statistical procedures such as in a t test are normally distributed.

Likert scale Named after Rensis Likert, scale used in surveys and questionnaires to simplify responses by providing from three to seven options in a consistent format (e.g., very dissatisfied, dissatisfied, no opinion, satisfied, very satisified).

Linear regression The use of correlation coefficients to plot a line illustrating the linear relationship of two variables x and y.

Longitudinal study A study that looks at phenomena over a period of time.

Mean The arithmetic average of a group of numbers.

Measures of central tendency Averages or values that represent what is typical for a group of values. The three major measures of central tendency are the mean, median, and mode.

Measures of relationship Statistical measures which show a relationship between two or more paired variables or two or more sets of data. The most common statistical measure of relationship is the correlation coefficient.

Measures of relative position Conversions of values to show where a given value stands in relation to other values of the same grouping. The most common example is the conversion of scores on standardized tests to show where a given student stands in relation to other students of the same age, grade level, etc. Sigma scores, College Board scores, percentiles, stanines, and standard scores are examples of converted test scores.

Measures of spread or dispersion Statistical measures which show contrasts or differences in a group of values. The most common measures of spread are the range, deviation, variance, and standard deviation.

Median The mid-point in a group of values, above and below which one-half of the values fall; a measure of central tendency.

Meta-analysis A study wherein a set of statistical procedures is used to summarize the results of a number of independently conducted research studies.

Mode The value in a group of values which occurs most often; a measure of central tendency.

Multiple regression A form of ANOVA which assumes there are three or more variables with one variable a dependent, interval or ratio variable and two or more, independent, interval or ratio variables such as test scores, incomes, grade-point average, etc. It is frequently used to develop prediction models.

Nondirectional hypothesis A hypothesis that makes no attempt to state either the direction or magnitude of what the researcher expects to find. An example of a nondirectional hypothesis is: "There is *no difference* in computer literacy between newly hired and experience teachers."

Nonparametric statistics Measures calculated for data that are not normally distributed.

Normal curve (Normal distribution) A distribution of values in a variable in which most values are near the mean and all values cluster around the mean in a symmetrical bell-shaped pattern. In a normal distribution the distance from one S.D. above the mean to one S.D. below the mean includes approximately 68 percent of all the values. Plus two to minus two S.D. includes approximately 95 percent of all values and plus three to minus three S.D. includes over 99 percent of all values.

Null hypothesis A hypothesis that is neither positive or negative and assumes a neutral position. See nondirectional hypothesis.

Parametric data Data which are measured and normally or near-normally distributed.

Parametric statistics Measures calculated for data that are assumed to be normally or near-normally distributed.

Pearson product moment coefficient (r) The most popular form of correlation coefficients used with two groups of continuous variables (e.g., test scores and grade-point averages).

Percentile rank A converted score which shows the point in a distribution below which a given percentage of scores fall. For example, if a score of 65 is at the seventieth percentile then 70 percent of the scores fall below 65.

Phi correlation coefficient (p) A form of the Pearson product moment coefficient that can be used with ordinal or ranked data.

Post hoc analysis Any procedure(s) used after an initial analysis to refine levels of statistical significance. For example, after an analysis of variance determines that two or more dependent groups are statistically different, a post hoc analysis could be used to determine which of the groups is statistically the most different. The Scheffe test, Fisher's LSD test, and Tukey's HSD test are examples of post hoc analysis procedures.

Predictor variable In prediction studies, the variable that predicts another variable. Also referred to as the independent variable.

Qualitative research A broad category of research that relies on narratives descriptions to study educational phenomena.

Quantitative research A broad category of research that relies on measurements and numerical data to study educational phenomena.

Random sampling The process of selecting a sample such that all the subjects in a population have an equal chance of being selected.

Range A measure of spread or dispersion which is the difference between the highest and lowest values in a group of values.

Reliability The degree to which a standardized test consistently measures what it is supposed to measure.

Research hypothesis A hypothesis in which the researcher states positively what he or she expects to find.

Research question A vehicle used to guide research, especially exploratory research that tends to be less specific than a hypothesis and leaves open an extension of the research depending upon the findings.

RIE Resources in Education.

Sample A smaller group of individuals or cases that is representative of a larger population.

Scientific method A procedure for problem-solving used in most disciplines which consists of four steps: defining a problem; stating a main question or hypothesis; collecting relevant data; and analyzing the data to answer the question or test the hypothesis.

Sigma (z) score The deviation from the mean divided by the standard deviation.

Significance level See *statistical significance.*

Spearman rank order coefficient A form of the Pearson product moment coefficient that can be used with categorical variables (e.g., pass/fail, male/female).

Standard deviation The most frequently used measure of spread or dispersion determined by calculating the square root of the variance. Abbrev.: S.D.

Standard error A statistical inference that assumes that the true measure (e.g., mean, correlation, difference of means) lies within a stipulated range above and below the value calculated for the measure.

Stanine A conversion of raw scores into nine bands or stanines, with the fifth stanine being at the mean, the first stanine containing the lowest, and the ninth stanine containing the highest.

Statistical significance An indication of the probability of a finding having occurred by chance; the general standard referred to as the .05 level of statistical significance indicates that the finding has a five percent (.05) chance of not being true and, conversely, a 95 percent chance of being true.

Statistics A body of mathematical techniques or processes for gathering, organizing, analyzing, and interpreting numerical data; the basic tools of measurement, evaluation, and research.

T score A variation of the sigma score which produces a standard score with a range of 20 to 80 and a mean of 50.

t test A parametric test used to determine the significance of the difference between the means of two groups of values.

Triangulation A multi-pronged approach to data collection which attempts to use one or more data-collection techniques to verify data collected by another technique.

Variable An item of data collected for each case in a study, and which varies or has more than one value.

Variance A commonly used measure of spread or dispersion calculated by the sum of all the squared deviations from the mean divided by the number (N) of values in the group.

Validity The degree to which a standardized test measures what it is supposed to measure.

z score See *Sigma score.*

Endnotes

1 INTRODUCTION

Gage, N. L. (1989), "The paradigm wars and their aftermath: A 'historical' sketch on research on teaching since 1989." *Teachers College Record*, 91(2): 133–150.

2 THE EDUCATIONAL RESEARCH OUTLINE AND THE SCIENTIFIC METHOD

Boeree, C. G. (1999), *Personality Traits: Jean Piaget 1896–1980.* <http://www.ship.edu/~cgboeree/piaget.html>
Wadsworth, B. J. (1996), *Piaget's Theory of Cognitive and Affective Development*, 5th edition. White Plains, NY: Longman Publishers.

3 RESOURCES AND TOOLS FOR DOING EDUCATIONAL RESEARCH

Clark, K. B. (1950), "Effect of prejudice and discrimination on personality development." Paper presented at the Midcentury White House Conference on Children and Youth, Washington, DC.
Kluger, R. (1975), *Simple Justice*. New York: Vintage Books.
Wiersma, W. (2000), *Research Methods in Education*, 7th edition. Boston: Allyn and Bacon.

4 QUALITATIVE METHODS: ETHNOGRAPHY, HISTORICAL RESEARCH, AND CASE STUDIES

Berg, B. L. (2004), *Qualitative Research Methods*, 5th edition. Boston: Pearson Education.
Lincoln, Yvonna S. (1986), "Negotiating politics in organizational cultures: some considerations for effective program evaluation." Paper delivered at the ASHE 1986 Annual Meeting. ERIC Document No. ED268893.

McDermott, R. (2001), "A century of Margaret Mead." *Teachers College Record*, **103**(5): 843–67.

Rogers, R. (2002), "Through the eyes of the institution: a critical discourse analysis of decision making in two special education meetings." *Anthropology & Education Quarterly* **33**(2): 213–37.

Walker, V. S. (1993), "Caswell County Training School, 1933–1969: relationship between community and school." *Harvard Education Review*, **63**(2): 161–82.

Walker, V. S. (1996), *Their Highest Potential: An African–American School Community in the Segregated South*. Chapel Hill, North Carolina: The University of North Carolina Press.

5 QUANTITATIVE METHODS: DESCRIPTIVE STUDIES, CORRELATION, AND CAUSAL-COMPARATIVE RESEARCH

Coleman, J. S., Campbell, E., Mood, A., Weinfeld, E., Hobson, D., York, R., and McPartland, J. (1966), *Equality of Educational Opportunity*. Washington, DC: Government Printing Office.

Jencks, C., Smith, M., Bane, M. J., Cohen, D., Gintis, H., Heyns, B., and Michelson, S. (1972), *Inequality: A Reassessment of the Effects of Family and Schooling in America*. New York: Basic Books.

McMillan, J. H. (2004), *Educational Research: Fundamentals for the Consumer*, 4th edition. Boston: Pearson Education, Allyn and Bacon.

6 EXPERIMENTAL STUDIES

Campbell, D. T. and Stanley J. C. (1963), "Experimental and quasi-experimental designs for research on teaching," in N. L. Gage (ed.), *Handbook of Research on Teaching* (pp. 171–246). Chicago: Rand McNally.

Cook, T. D. (2002), "Randomized experiments in educational policy research: a critical examination of the reasons the educational evaluation community has offered for not doing them." *Educational Evaluation & Policy Analysis*, **24**(3): 175–99.

Gay, L. R. (1992), *Educational Research: Competencies for Analysis and Application*, 4th edition. New York: Merrill.

Gorard, S. (2001), *Quantitative Methods in Educational Research*. London: Continuum.

McMillan, J. H. (2004), *Educational Research: Fundamentals for the Consumer*, 4th Edition. Boston: Pearson Education, Allyn and Bacon.

Slavin, R. E. (1979), "Effects of biracial learning teams on cross racial friendships." *Journal of Educational Psychology*, **71**(3): 381–7.

Slavin, R. E. (1992), *Research Methods in Education*. Boston: Allyn and Bacon.

Wiersma, W. (2000), *Research Methods in Education: An Introduction*, 7th edition. Boston. Allyn and Bacon.

7 ACTION AND EVALUATION RESEARCH

Charles, C. M. and Mertler, C. A. (2002), *Introduction to Educational Research*, 4th edition. New York: Allyn and Bacon.

Gay, L. R. (1992), *Educational Research: Competencies for Analysis and Application*, 4th edition. New York: Merrill.

Gorard, S. (2002), *Quantitative Methods in Educational Research*. London: Continuum.

McMillan, J. H. (2004), *Educational Research: Fundamentals for the Consumer*, 4th edition. Boston: Pearson Education, Allyn and Bacon.

Mosteller, F. (1999), "The case for smaller classes and for what works in the schoolroom." *Harvard Magazine*, May/June 1999.
< http://www.harvard-magazine.com/issues/mj99/forum.html >

Sagor, R. (2000), *Guiding School Improvement with Action Research*, 4th edition. Alexandria, VA: Association for Supervision and Curriculum Development.

Slavin, R. E. (1992), *Research Methods in Education*. Boston: Allyn and Bacon.

Word, E., Johnston, J., Bain, H., Fulton, D. B., Boyd-Zaharias, J., Lintz, M. N., Achilles, C. M., Folger, J., and Breda, C. (1990), *Student/Teacher Achievement Ratio (STAR): Tennessee's K-3 Class–Size Study*. Nashville, TN: Tennessee Department of Education. < http://www.cde.ca.gov/classsize/eval/projstar.htm >

8 SHARING RESULTS: THE RESEARCH REPORT

American Psychological Association (latest edition), *Publication Manual of the American Psychological Association*. Washington, DC: author.

Beck, C. L. and Gargiulo, R. M. (1983), "Burnout in teachers of retarded and nonretarded children." *Journal of Educational Research*, **76**(2): 169–73.

Stempien, L. R. and Loeb, R. C. (2002), "Differences in job satisfaction between general education and special education teachers: Implications for retention." *Remedial and Special Education*, **23**(5): 258–67.

Strunk, Jr., W. and White, E. B. (latest edition), *Elements of Style*. Upper Saddle River, NJ: Pearson Education/Longman.

Wisniewski, L. and Gargiulo, R. (1997), "Occupational stress and burnout among special educators: a review of the literature." *The Journal of Special Education*, **31**(4): 325–46.

Index